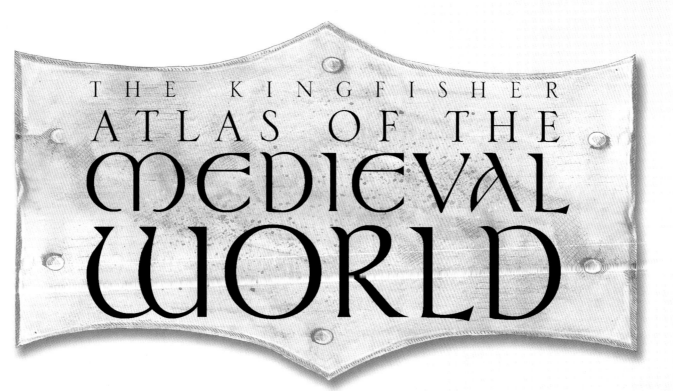

THE KINGFISHER
ATLAS OF THE
MEDIEVAL WORLD

Simon Adams

Illustrated by Kevin Maddison

KINGFISHER

BOSTON

KINGFISHER

a Houghton Mifflin Company imprint
222 Berkeley Street
Boston, MA 02116
www.houghtonmifflinbooks.com

Senior editor: Simon Holland
Coordinating editors: Sarah Snavely, Caitlin Doyle
Designers: Jack Clucas, Mike Davis, Dominic Zwemmer
Cover designers: Malcolm Parchment, Poppy Jenkins
Consultant: Professor Norman Housley, University of Leicester, U.K.
Picture research manager: Cee Weston-Baker
Senior production controller: Jessamy Oldfield
DTP coordinator: Catherine Hibbert
Indexer: Catherine Brereton
Proofreader: Ronne Randall

Cartography by: Colin and Ian McCarthy
                   Maidenhead Cartographic Services Limited,
                   Maidenhead, Berkshire, U.K.

First published in 2006
10 9 8 7 6 5 4 3 2

2TR/0407/SHENS/CLSN/158MA/C

ISBN: 978-0-7534-5946-1

LIBRARY OF CONGRESS CATALOGING-IN-PUBLICATION DATA
Adams, Simon, 1955–
  The Kingfisher atlas of the medieval world / Simon Adams.—1st ed.
    p. cm.
Includes index.
1. Civilization, Medieval—Juvenile literature. 2. Middle Ages—Juvenile literature.
  I. Title.
CB351.A23 2007
909.07—dc22   2006005554

Printed in Taiwan

CONTENTS

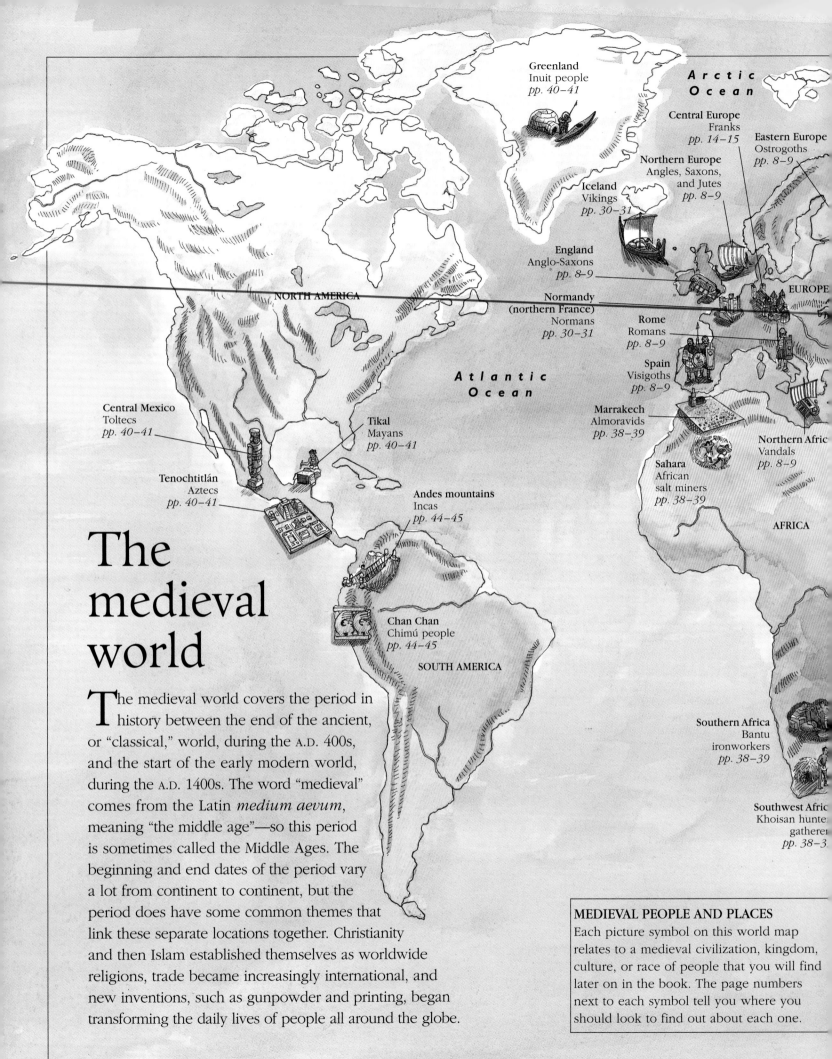

Greenland
Inuit people
pp. 40–41

Arctic Ocean

Central Europe
Franks
pp. 14–15

Eastern Europe
Ostrogoths
pp. 8–9

Northern Europe
Angles, Saxons,
and Jutes
pp. 8–9

Iceland
Vikings
pp. 30–31

EUROPE

England
Anglo-Saxons
pp. 8–9

NORTH AMERICA

Normandy
(northern France)
Normans
pp. 30–31

Rome
Romans
pp. 8–9

Atlantic Ocean

Spain
Visigoths
pp. 8–9

Central Mexico
Toltecs
pp. 40–41

Marrakech
Almoravids
pp. 38–39

Northern Afric
Vandals
pp. 8–9

Tikal
Mayans
pp. 40–41

Sahara
African
salt miners
pp. 38–39

Tenochtitlán
Aztecs
pp. 40–41

Andes mountains
Incas
pp. 44–45

AFRICA

Chan Chan
Chimú people
pp. 44–45

SOUTH AMERICA

Southern Africa
Bantu
ironworkers
pp. 38–39

The medieval world

The medieval world covers the period in
history between the end of the ancient,
or "classical," world, during the A.D. 400s,
and the start of the early modern world,
during the A.D. 1400s. The word "medieval"
comes from the Latin *medium aevum*,
meaning "the middle age"—so this period
is sometimes called the Middle Ages. The
beginning and end dates of the period vary
a lot from continent to continent, but the
period does have some common themes that
link these separate locations together. Christianity
and then Islam established themselves as worldwide
religions, trade became increasingly international, and
new inventions, such as gunpowder and printing, began
transforming the daily lives of people all around the globe.

Southwest Afric
Khoisan hunte
gatherer
pp. 38–3

MEDIEVAL PEOPLE AND PLACES

Each picture symbol on this world map
relates to a medieval civilization, kingdom,
culture, or race of people that you will find
later on in the book. The page numbers
next to each symbol tell you where you
should look to find out about each one.

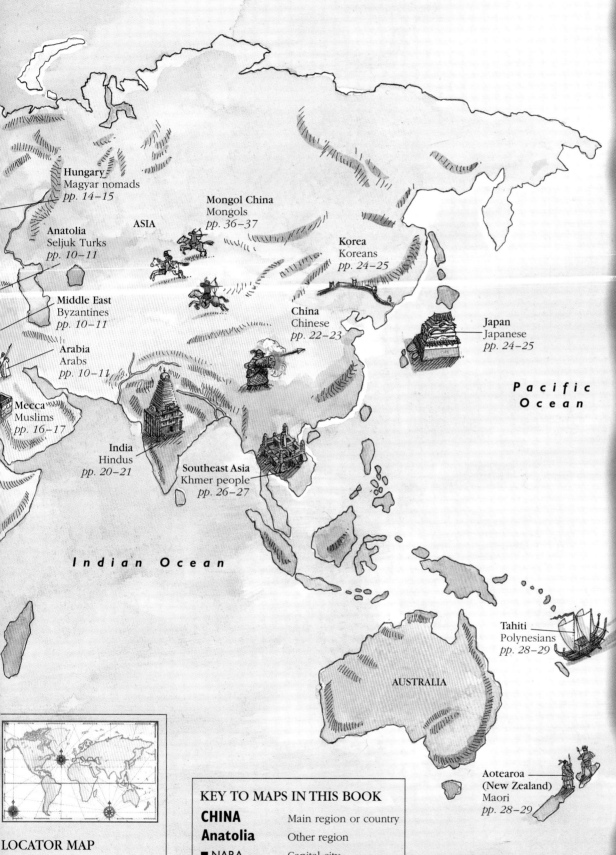

Hungary
Magyar nomads
pp. 14–15

Anatolia
Seljuk Turks
pp. 10–11

ASIA

Mongol China
Mongols
pp. 36–37

Korea
Koreans
pp. 24–25

Middle East
Byzantines
pp. 10–11

Arabia
Arabs
pp. 10–11

China
Chinese
pp. 22–23

Japan
Japanese
pp. 24–25

Mecca
Muslims
pp. 16–17

India
Hindus
pp. 20–21

Southeast Asia
Khmer people
pp. 26–27

Pacific
Ocean

Indian Ocean

AUSTRALIA

Tahiti
Polynesians
pp. 28–29

Aotearoa
(New Zealand)
Maori
pp. 28–29

LOCATOR MAP

You will find a diagram like this along with every map in the book. This allows you to see exactly which part of the world the main map is showing you.

KEY TO MAPS IN THIS BOOK

CHINA	Main region or country
Anatolia	Other region
■ NARA	Capital city
● Tikal	City, town, or village
Rhine	River or lake
Himalayas	Ocean, sea, desert, or mountain range
– – – –	Empire boundary

A.D. 500

527 Emperor Justinian rules eastern Roman Empire and regains territory lost to barbarian control
550 Slav peoples settle in eastern Europe
589 China reunited under Sui and Tang dynasties after long period of conflict

A.D. 600

600 Frankish kingdom becomes the most powerful state in western Europe
610 Eastern Roman Empire becomes the Byzantine Empire
622 Muhammad flees from Mecca to Medina: the birth of Islam
632 Death of Muhammad: rapid expansion of Islam
680 Islam split between Sunni and Shia Muslims

A.D. 700

711 Arabs invade Spain

732 Invading Arab army defeated by the Franks at Poitiers in France

750 Abbasids rule Muslim world from Baghdad

793 Vikings raid western Europe for the first time

A.D. 800

800 Charlemagne crowned Emperor of the Romans by the Pope in Rome
802 Creation of Khmer Empire in Cambodia, Southeast Asia
850 Chinese first use gunpowder in warfare
850 Chimú Empire founded in South America
868 World's first book printed in China

A.D. 900

936 Korea emerges as a unified nation

962 Holy Roman Empire created in Germany and Italy

A.D. 1000

c. 1000 Polynesian navigators reach New Zealand
1000 Easter Islanders begin carving stone statues
1000 Vikings settle in North America
1054 Final split between the Roman and Orthodox churches
1066 Norman conquest of England
1095 First Crusade to win back the Holy Land from Muslim control

A.D. 1100

1171 England first rules Ireland
1175 Muslim conquest of northern India begins

1192 Military shogun government rules Japan

A.D. 1200

c. 1200 Great Zimbabwe founded
1206 Genghis Khan begins Mongol conquests
1220 Inca Empire founded
1241 Mongols invade eastern Europe
1250 Kingdom of Benin founded in West Africa
1279 Mongols conquer China
1280 Ottoman Empire founded
1291 Muslims expel crusaders from Holy Land

A.D. 1300

1325 Aztec Empire founded
1337 England and France begin the Hundred Years' War
1347 Black Death starts to overwhelm Europe
1354 Ottomans begin conquest of the Balkans
1361 Timur creates new Mongol Empire in central Asia
1368 Ming dynasty ends Mongol rule of China

A.D. 1400

1415 Portuguese establish their first European colony in Africa
1432 Portuguese begin exploring West African coast

A.D. 1500

The medieval world:
How we know about the past

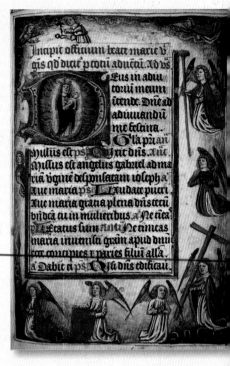

The medieval world came to an end more than 500 years ago, but evidence from the period is all around us today. Medieval towns and castles, churches and cathedrals, temples and mosques, books and documents, ships and wagons, artifacts and jewelry, as well as many other things, still survive. These remains enable us to build up a good picture of what it was like to live and work all those years ago, while examining them can reveal how things were constructed in medieval times. We can also use documents from the period to reenact festivals, battles, and famous events.

Medieval towns

Many of the walled towns built during the medieval period still survive. Owing to careful restoration in the 1800s, Carcassonne in France (shown below) is a perfect example. Its castle, walls, gatehouses, and street plan are almost untouched since the town was fortified during the 1200s.

Town walls are 4,200 feet (1,280m) long and include three gatehouses and 21 towers.

Documents

Medieval books and paper documents are rare. The Chinese had printing presses, but European monks and scholars had to write each book out by hand, adding beautiful illustrations

Reconstructions

Wooden artifacts can easily rot away. Luckily, this Viking ship from Oseberg in Norway was buried in boggy clay soil, which preserved most of its timbers. This allowed archaeologists to have the ship rebuilt to its original design.

Excavations

This medieval ship (above) was found buried in a muddy river in Newport, Wales, U.K. Every piece of timber and scrap of evidence was examined to build up an almost complete picture of how wooden trading ships were designed and built during this period.

Artifacts

This limestone figure from Central America is of Chicomecoatl, the Mayan goddess of maize. It also shows us the clothing and jewelry that an ordinary Mayan woman of the period might have worn.

Reenactments

We cannot go back in time to fight a joust or win a battle, but we can reenact them using medieval accounts as our guide. These jousters are taking part in a medieval fair staged in Sarasota, Florida. Their costumes and weapons are modern re-creations of the medieval originals.

After the Roman Empire

The mighty Roman Empire had dominated Europe for more than 500 years, but during the A.D. 400s, it slowly fell apart, as waves of Germanic tribes from central Europe poured over its borders. The western half of the empire finally collapsed in A.D. 476, when the last western emperor, Augustulus, was overthrown. In its place came a series of tribal kingdoms that converted to Christianity and kept many of the old Roman institutions in place.

St. Patrick
In 432 St. Patrick arrived in Ireland to convert its people to Christianity.

Anglo-Saxons
Angles, Saxons, and Jutes from northern Germany and Denmark crossed the North Sea to settle in eastern Britain after 450.

Barbarians
There were many "barbarian" tribes in Germany, but most of them were helpful to the Romans.

Sutton Hoo
Anglo-Saxon lords were buried in their ships surrounded by treasures such as this helmet from Sutton Hoo.

Theodoric
In 493 Theodoric, king of the Ostrogoths, conquered Rome and restored peace, keeping Roman civilization alive in Italy.

The Visigoths
The Visigoths came from the Balkans, and in 418 they settled in southwestern France as allies of Rome. They later conquered much of Spain.

Attacking Rome
Rome was ransacked by the Visigoths in 410 and then by the Vandals in 455.

The Vandals
The Vandals from central Europe crossed over to North Africa and set up an independent kingdom in Carthage in 439.

Vandal pirates
Vandal pirates from North Africa attacked Roman ships in the Mediterranean, seizing valuable cargoes.

Ireland

Britain

North Sea

Rhine

Germany

Gaul
Wooden houses

Alps

Ruined Roman villa

Suevic Kingdom

Spain

Visigothic kingdom

Atlantic Ocean

Buildings in Ravenna

Ravenna

Kingdom of Odoacer

ROME

WESTERN ROMAN EMPIRE

Vandal kingdom

Carthage

North Africa

dotted line shows the extent of the Roman Empire in the A.D. 400s

The Slavs
No one knows where the Slavs came from, but during the 500s, they settled across eastern Europe, later converting to Christianity.

The Ostrogoths
The Ostrogoths settled in the Balkans and eventually conquered Italy itself. They often helped Rome against its enemies.

Balkans

The legacy of Rome
The Roman Empire left behind many achievements. The Romans introduced the calendar of 365 days—with an extra day every four years—devised by Julius Caesar in 45 B.C. This system included the 12-month year, the seven-day week, and the names of our months. October is shown on this mosaic floor from the A.D. 200s. Other Roman legacies include the Catholic Church, the Latin language, a legal system, and a system of republican government that has been copied in modern France and the U.S.

Constantinople
The eastern empire was governed from Constantinople. The city's massive walls kept it free from attacks.

■ CONSTANTINOPLE

Black Sea

EASTERN ROMAN EMPIRE

Anatolia

Athens

SASSANIAN EMPIRE

Mediterranean Sea

0   500km
0   250 miles

Arabs
The eastern borders of the Roman Empire were not threatened as often as those in the north, as the Arabs traded peacefully with the Romans. The Sassanian Persians, however, were a constant threat.

A.D. 400

402 Capital of the western empire moves from Rome to the safer city of Ravenna
406 Vandals, Suevi, and Alans invade Gaul (France) and later Spain
410 Visigoths ransack Rome
418 Visigoths make peace with Rome and settle in Aquitaine (southwestern France)

429 Vandals cross from Spain to North Africa and conquer Carthage in 439
432 St. Patrick begins converting the Irish to Christianity

A.D. 450

450 Anglo-Saxons from northern Germany begin settling in Britain
455 Vandals ransack Rome

476 Odoacer, a barbarian general, removes the last western Roman emperor, Augustulus, from power and rules Italy

486 Clovis founds the Frankish kingdom in Gaul

493–526 Theodoric rules Ostrogothic kingdom in Italy

A.D. 500

507 Clovis drives the Visigoths out of Gaul and into Spain

527–565 Justinian rules eastern Roman Empire and reconquers much of the land lost to the barbarians

A.D. 550

550 Slavs settle in eastern Europe and the Balkans

570s Visigoths dominate most of Spain

A.D. 600

600 Frankish kingdom becomes the most powerful state in western Europe

626 Avar nomadic tribes threaten the eastern empire but fail to take Constantinople

639 After death of King Dagobert, a sequence of short-lived kings weakens the Frankish kingdom

A.D. 650

679 Pepin II leads the Frankish kingdom and expands Frankish power into Germany

A.D. 700

Byzantine architecture
The Byzantines developed a distinctive style of church architecture, using domes and mosaic walls. An example is the Basilica of St. Mark in Venice.

Craftsmen making a mosaic on a wall

Missionaries
In 863 Byzantine missionaries, Saints Cyril and Methodius, set out to convert the pagan Slavs of eastern Europe to Christianity.

Frontier forts
Justinian built a series of forts along the Danube to protect his frontier against attacks by Slav raiders.

Emperor Justinian
Justinian fought to regain Roman lands lost to the barbarians.

Byzantine priest

Byzantine-style Christian church

The Normans
In 1091 Norman knights from France conquered Byzantine lands in southern Italy and Sicily.

Mount Athos
Communities of religious men, such as the one on Mount Athos, sprang up across the Byzantine Empire.

dotted line shows the extent of the Byzantine Empire in 1025

Constantinople
The Byzantine capital of Constantinople was founded in 324 by the Roman Emperor Constantine.

Myriocepha
Farmer taking goat to the mar

Venice

Ravenna

Italy

Rome

Bari

Sicily

Danube

Black Sea

Bulgaria

Balathista

Adrianople

CONSTANTINOPLE

Thessalonica

Mount Athos

Nicaea

Ephesus

BYZANTINE EMPIRE

Crete

Mediterranean Sea

The Byzantine Empire

Despite the collapse of the western Roman Empire in A.D. 476, the eastern empire continued to prosper. During the reign of Justinian (527–565), it even managed to regain land that was lost to the barbarians. But the empire was threatened by enemies all along its lengthy borders, so Heraclius (reigned 610–641) completely restructured the empire and changed its official language from Latin to Greek. He created a new "Byzantine Empire"—named after its capital city, Byzantium—the old Greek name for Constantinople. This new empire survived against its many enemies until 1453, when Constantinople finally fell to the Ottoman Turks.

Muslim rule
Arab armies swept out of Arabia in 632, bringing their new religion, Islam. Islam replaced Christianity throughout the eastern half of the empire.

Egypt

Newly built mosque in Egypt

0		500km
0		250 miles

Arab threat
Arab armies regularly threatened the empire, invading Byzantine lands and twice besieging the capital, Constantinople.

Armenia
Armenia, the oldest Christian nation, joined the Byzantine Empire in 1020, seeking protection from its Muslim neighbors.

"Greek fire"
In 677 a Syrian named Kallinikos invented a mixture that burned on contact with water. It was used to destroy the Arab fleet besieging Constantinople.

ARMENIA

Trebizond

Manzikert

Seljuk Turks
In 1071 the Seljuk Turks achieved a great victory over the Byzantines at Manzikert and conquered most of Anatolia.

Anatolia

Two-story life
Most Byzantine farmhouses had two stories, with animals stabled on the ground floor and people living above them.

Cyprus

Merchant ship in eastern Mediterranean

Syria

Jerusalem

Palestine

Yarmuk river
In 635 Muslim-Arab armies defeated the Byzantines along the Yarmuk river, going on to conquer all of Syria and Palestine.

Arabia

Orthodox Christianity
After the division of the Roman Empire in 395, the Patriarch (leader of the Orthodox Church in Constantinople) and the Pope (leader of the Catholic Church in Rome) steadily grew apart. Both claimed supremacy over each other, and their two churches differed increasingly. These differences became a split in 1054 during the reign of Emperor Constantine IX, who is shown on the left in this mosaic (above). From then on the two churches were often bitter enemies, only settling their differences in 1965.

A.D. 500

527–565 Justinian restores Roman power in the Mediterranean by reconquering Italy, southern Spain, and North Africa

A.D. 600

607–627 War against the Sassanian Persians, ending in Byzantine victory
638 Arabs capture Jerusalem and the rest of Palestine and Syria
640–698 Arabs conquer Byzantine North Africa
670–677 Arabs besiege Constantinople

A.D. 700

716–717 Arabs again fail to capture Constantinople

A.D. 800

860 Rus (Swedish Viking) raiders attack Constantinople
863 Saints Cyril and Methodius begin converting pagan Slavs to Christianity

A.D. 900

963 First monasteries built at Mount Athos

A.D. 1000

1018 Emperor Basil II conquers Bulgaria and extends northern frontier up to the Danube
1054 Serious disagreement between Orthodox and Catholic churches
1071 Seljuk Turks defeat Byzantines at Manzikert
1099 First Christian Crusade from western Europe recaptures Jerusalem from Muslim control

A.D. 1100

1176 Seljuk Turks inflict another crushing defeat over the Byzantines at Myriocephalum in Anatolia

A.D. 1200

1204 Fourth Crusade captures Constantinople, seriously weakening the empire

1261 Byzantines retake Constantinople

1280 Ottoman Turkish state founded in Anatolia

A.D. 1300

1354 Ottomans cross into Europe and surround Constantinople

A.D. 1400

1453 Ottomans capture Constantinople, bringing Byzantine Empire to an end

A.D. 1500

Monasteries
These are the remains of Fountains Abbey in Yorkshire, England—once part of a large monastic estate that was founded by 13 Benedictine monks in 1132. Monasteries were major centers of learning and scholarship across Europe, running schools to provide education for boys.

Pilgrimage
The pilgrimage was an important part of medieval Christianity. Both rich and poor walked to shrines, such as Canterbury in England, Santiago de Compostela in Spain, Rome, and even Jerusalem, in search of a miraculous cure or forgiveness for their sins. This stained-glass window from Canterbury cathedral shows pilgrims on their way to the shrine of St. Thomas à Becket.

Medieval Europe:
Christianity

Medieval Europe was entirely Christian, with the exception of southern Spain, and after the 1300s, the Balkans. In the west of Europe the Catholic Church played a major role in society, providing schools and hospitals and encouraging people to make pilgrimages to holy places or shrines containing relics of saints. The Catholic Church also dominated politics and owned large areas of land. The Pope, based in Rome, was the head of the Catholic Church. He was often more powerful than most emperors and kings, although disputes between himself and these nonreligious leaders often led to bitter arguments, and even war.

Christian education
The Christian Church played a major role in education across Europe, as priests and monks—such as those shown in this illuminated manuscript—were often the only people in the area who could read and write. Churches and cathedrals ran their own schools, and after the A.D. 1000s many cathedral schools set up universities to teach theology (the study of religious belief) and law.

Taller spire added in
the early 1500s

West front survives from an
earlier 11th-century cathedral,
destroyed by a fire in 1194

Stained-glass rose
window showing
religious scenes

Brightly painted interior

The Orthodox Church
Most people in eastern Europe
were Orthodox Christians under
the leadership of the Patriarch
of Constantinople rather than
the Catholic Pope in Rome. In
the 1300s—when this monastery
was built in Kosovo, Serbia—
most Orthodox Christians
outside of Russia and Georgia
came under Ottoman Muslim
rule, but they continued
practicing their faith.

Flying buttress to
support the walls
and roof

Central part of cathedral,
the nave, is 121 feet
(37m) high

Sculptures on south
porch depict New
Testament scenes

Part of the front section is
pulled away in this drawing
to reveal the interior

Chartres cathedral
The largest building in any medieval European city was the
cathedral, the seat of the local bishop. Constructing a cathedral
employed hundreds of local stonemasons, carpenters, sculptors,
and glassmakers. The cathedral in Chartres, southwest of Paris,
France, was begun in the early 1200s and only took 25 years to
build. It has remained largely untouched since 1250, making it
one of the finest surviving medieval cathedrals in existence.

Charlemagne's Europe

In A.D. 711 Muslim armies from North Africa crossed into Europe and soon conquered Visigothic Spain. The Franks now ruled over the only surviving Germanic kingdom in Europe. Yet, the Franks were weak, because whenever a king died, it was their custom to divide up the kingdom among all the king's sons. So when Pepin III died in 768, his kingdom was divided between his sons Carloman and Charlemagne. Carloman died three years later, leaving Charlemagne in control. For 30 years, Charlemagne campaigned to extend his kingdom, establishing a new Roman Empire that covered most of western Europe.

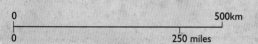

0   500km
0   250 miles

Charlemagne's empire
Charlemagne governed his empire from his palace in Aachen (right). From there, he sent out a stream of orders and instructions that provided a model of how a good king should rule. He also set up systems of government for Europe that were to last for the next 700 years. Charlemagne could barely read or write, but he provided funds to support and encourage learning in his empire.

Ireland

Viking wooden houses in Dublin

Offa's dyke
In the late 700s King Offa of Mercia built a huge dirt and timber rampart along his western boundary to keep out the hostile Welsh.

W

WE

Atlantic Ocean

Brittany

dotted line shows the extent of the Frankish kingdom in around 814

Poitiers
In 732 the leader of the Franks defeated a large Muslim army at Poitiers. From then on, the Muslims were in retreat in western Europe.

Charlemagne's royal seal

Covadonga

Trading ship

Christian church

Spain

Córdoba
Córdoba, the capital of Muslim Spain, was the biggest city in Europe during the time of Charlemagne, with a population of more than 100,000.

UMAYYAD CALIPHATE

Córdoba

The Holy Roman Empire
On Christmas Day in 800, Charlemagne was crowned Emperor of the Romans by the Pope in Rome (above). He became a Christian successor to the emperors of ancient Rome. His empire broke up after his death, and in 911 the Saxon dynasty took power in East Francia (Germany). Otto I (ruled 936–973) expanded his kingdom by defeating the Magyars and the Slavs and by conquering Burgundy, Provence, and Italy. In 962 the Pope crowned Otto as Holy Roman Emperor.

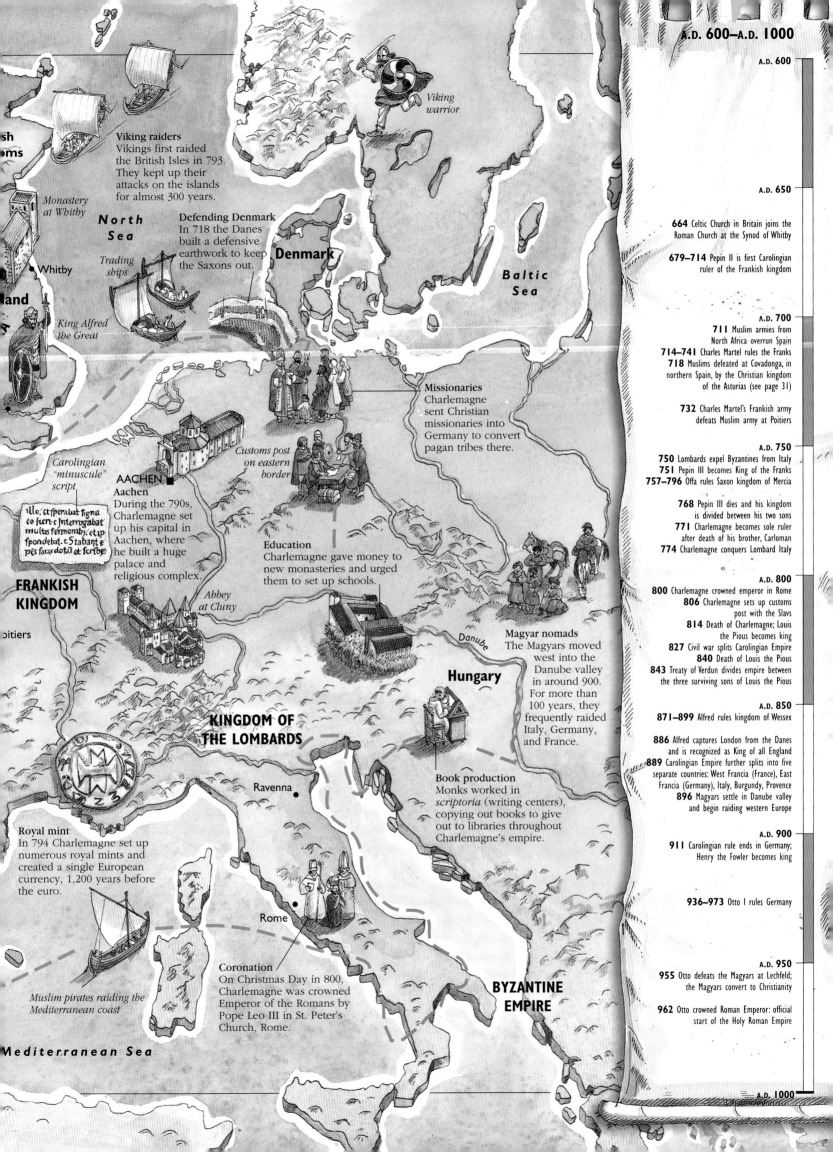

Viking raiders
Vikings first raided the British Isles in 793. They kept up their attacks on the islands for almost 300 years.

Viking warrior

Monastery at Whitby

North Sea

• Whitby

Trading ships

Defending Denmark
In 718 the Danes built a defensive earthwork to keep the Saxons out.

Denmark

Baltic Sea

King Alfred the Great

Carolingian "minuscule" script

AACHEN ■
Aachen
During the 790s, Charlemagne set up his capital in Aachen, where he built a huge palace and religious complex.

Customs post on eastern border

Missionaries
Charlemagne sent Christian missionaries into Germany to convert pagan tribes there.

Education
Charlemagne gave money to new monasteries and urged them to set up schools.

FRANKISH KINGDOM

oitiers

Abbey at Cluny

Danube

Magyar nomads
The Magyars moved west into the Danube valley in around 900. For more than 100 years, they frequently raided Italy, Germany, and France.

Hungary

KINGDOM OF THE LOMBARDS

Ravenna •

Book production
Monks worked in *scriptoria* (writing centers), copying out books to give out to libraries throughout Charlemagne's empire.

Royal mint
In 794 Charlemagne set up numerous royal mints and created a single European currency, 1,200 years before the euro.

Rome •

Coronation
On Christmas Day in 800, Charlemagne was crowned Emperor of the Romans by Pope Leo III in St. Peter's Church, Rome.

Muslim pirates raiding the Mediterranean coast

BYZANTINE EMPIRE

Mediterranean Sea

(see page 31)

A.D. 600–A.D. 1000

A.D. 600

A.D. 650

664 Celtic Church in Britain joins the Roman Church at the Synod of Whitby

679–714 Pepin II is first Carolingian ruler of the Frankish kingdom

A.D. 700

711 Muslim armies from North Africa overrun Spain
714–741 Charles Martel rules the Franks
718 Muslims defeated at Covadonga, in northern Spain, by the Christian kingdom of the Asturias (see page 31)

732 Charles Martel's Frankish army defeats Muslim army at Poitiers

A.D. 750

750 Lombards expel Byzantines from Italy
751 Pepin III becomes King of the Franks
757–796 Offa rules Saxon kingdom of Mercia

768 Pepin III dies and his kingdom is divided between his two sons
771 Charlemagne becomes sole ruler after death of his brother, Carloman
774 Charlemagne conquers Lombard Italy

A.D. 800

800 Charlemagne crowned emperor in Rome
806 Charlemagne sets up customs post with the Slavs
814 Death of Charlemagne; Louis the Pious becomes king
827 Civil war splits Carolingian Empire
840 Death of Louis the Pious
843 Treaty of Verdun divides empire between the three surviving sons of Louis the Pious

A.D. 850

871–899 Alfred rules kingdom of Wessex

886 Alfred captures London from the Danes and is recognized as King of all England
889 Carolingian Empire further splits into five separate countries: West Francia (France), East Francia (Germany), Italy, Burgundy, Provence
896 Magyars settle in Danube valley and begin raiding western Europe

A.D. 900

911 Carolingian rule ends in Germany; Henry the Fowler becomes king

936–973 Otto I rules Germany

A.D. 950

955 Otto defeats the Magyars at Lechfeld; the Magyars convert to Christianity

962 Otto crowned Roman Emperor: official start of the Holy Roman Empire

A.D. 1000

Battle of Poitiers
In 732 Arab armies invaded France, reaching as far north as Poitiers. There, they were defeated by a large Frankish army.

Poitiers

FRANKISH KINGDOM

Constantinople
Despite their many successes, the Arabs twice failed to capture Constantinople, the capital of the Byzantine Empire.

Constantinople

UMAYYAD CALIPHATE

Córdoba
From 756 to 1031 the Umayyads governed Spain from Córdoba, where they built a beautiful mosque. This mihrab from the mosque shows the direction of Mecca.

CÓRDOBA

Rome

Anatolia

Taurus Mountains

BYZANTINE EMPIRE

Carthage

IDRISID CALIPHATE

AGHLABID CALIPHATE

S

DAM

Pale

Jer

Jerusalem
In 638 Arab armies captured Jerusalem and built the Dome of the Rock—the first major Islamic building outside Arabia.

Arabic
The Arab armies introduced a new language, Arabic, across their vast empire. Spoken Arabic varies from country to country, but written Arabic is the same everywhere.

Muslim raiders
Muslim pirates launched frequent raids across the Mediterranean, capturing Sicily, Sardinia, and other islands.

Libya

North Africa

Cairo

Egypt

Camel

Cairo
The Fatimid rulers of Egypt established a new city at Cairo in 969. It soon became one of the most important cities in the Arab world.

A Muslim praying toward Mecca

Nile

Felucca on the Nile river

The spread of Islam

In A.D. 610 Muhammad, a trader from Mecca in Arabia, began experiencing divine revelations that were later written down in the Koran, the Islamic holy book. By the time of his death in 632, the new religion of Islam dominated the Arabian peninsula. Arab armies then set out on a whirlwind campaign of conquest and conversion. They overwhelmed the Sassanian Empire of Persia and took Islam from the borders of India across Asia and North Africa into Spain and southern Europe. Islam brought political and religious unity to a vast region, but divisions soon opened up. Weakened by these divisions, the Islamic world lost some of its territory to Christian forces in Europe.

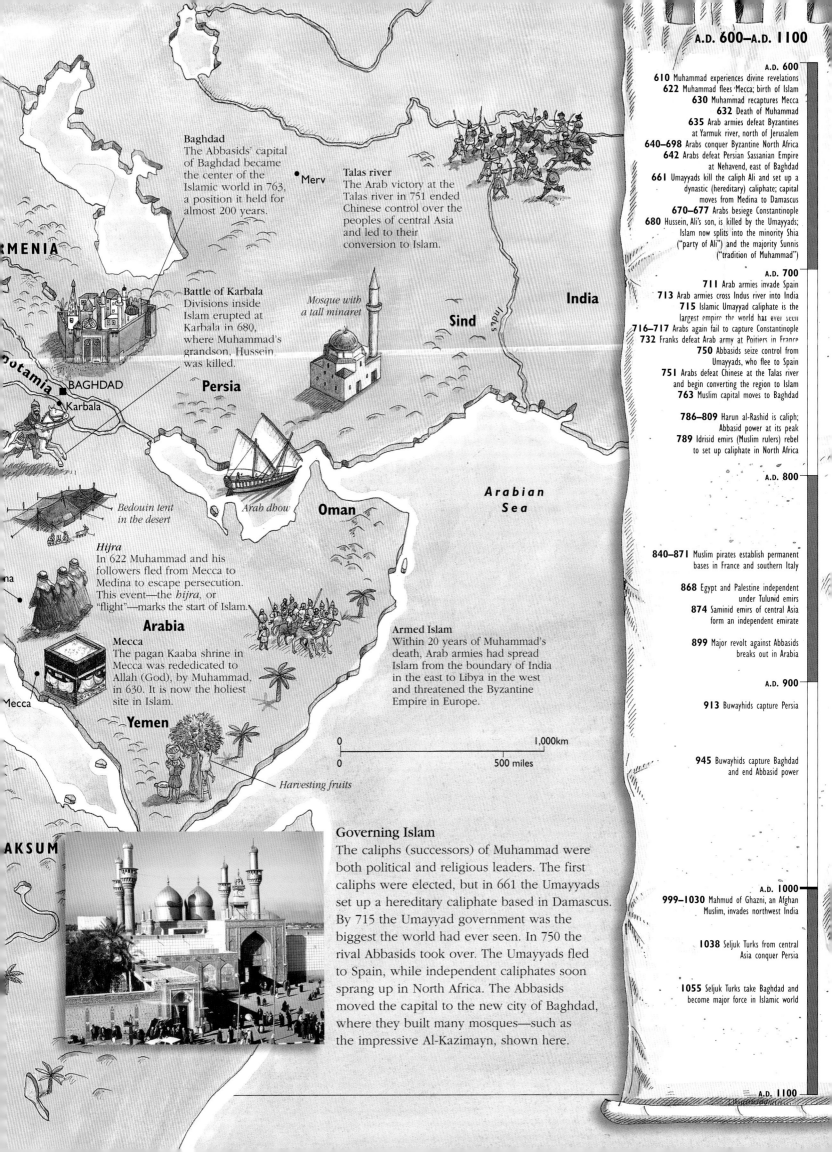

Baghdad
The Abbasids' capital of Baghdad became the center of the Islamic world in 763, a position it held for almost 200 years.

• Merv

Talas river
The Arab victory at the Talas river in 751 ended Chinese control over the peoples of central Asia and led to their conversion to Islam.

ARMENIA

Battle of Karbala
Divisions inside Islam erupted at Karbala in 680, where Muhammad's grandson, Hussein was killed.

Mosque with a tall minaret

India

Sind

...otamia

BAGHDAD

Karbala

Persia

Bedouin tent in the desert

Arab dhow

Oman

Arabian Sea

Hijra
In 622 Muhammad and his followers fled from Mecca to Medina to escape persecution. This event—the *hijra*, or "flight"—marks the start of Islam.

...na

Arabia

Mecca
The pagan Kaaba shrine in Mecca was rededicated to Allah (God), by Muhammad, in 630. It is now the holiest site in Islam.

Mecca

Armed Islam
Within 20 years of Muhammad's death, Arab armies had spread Islam from the boundary of India in the east to Libya in the west and threatened the Byzantine Empire in Europe.

Yemen

0 ————————————— 1,000km

0 ————————————— 500 miles

Harvesting fruits

AKSUM

Governing Islam

The caliphs (successors) of Muhammad were both political and religious leaders. The first caliphs were elected, but in 661 the Umayyads set up a hereditary caliphate based in Damascus. By 715 the Umayyad government was the biggest the world had ever seen. In 750 the rival Abbasids took over. The Umayyads fled to Spain, while independent caliphates soon sprang up in North Africa. The Abbasids moved the capital to the new city of Baghdad, where they built many mosques—such as the impressive Al-Kazimayn, shown here.

A.D. 600
610 Muhammad experiences divine revelations
622 Muhammad flees Mecca; birth of Islam
630 Muhammad recaptures Mecca
632 Death of Muhammad
635 Arab armies defeat Byzantines at Yarmuk river, north of Jerusalem
640–698 Arabs conquer Byzantine North Africa
642 Arabs defeat Persian Sassanian Empire at Nehavend, east of Baghdad
661 Umayyads kill the caliph Ali and set up a dynastic (hereditary) caliphate; capital moves from Medina to Damascus
670–677 Arabs besiege Constantinople
680 Hussein, Ali's son, is killed by the Umayyads; Islam now splits into the minority Shia ("party of Ali") and the majority Sunnis ("tradition of Muhammad")

A.D. 700
711 Arab armies invade Spain
713 Arab armies cross Indus river into India
715 Islamic Umayyad caliphate is the largest empire the world has ever seen
716–717 Arabs again fail to capture Constantinople
732 Franks defeat Arab army at Poitiers in France
750 Abbasids seize control from Umayyads, who flee to Spain
751 Arabs defeat Chinese at the Talas river and begin converting the region to Islam
763 Muslim capital moves to Baghdad

786–809 Harun al-Rashid is caliph; Abbasid power at its peak
789 Idrisid emirs (Muslim rulers) rebel to set up caliphate in North Africa

A.D. 800

840–871 Muslim pirates establish permanent bases in France and southern Italy

868 Egypt and Palestine independent under Tulunid emirs
874 Samanid emirs of central Asia form an independent emirate

899 Major revolt against Abbasids breaks out in Arabia

A.D. 900

913 Buwayhids capture Persia

945 Buwayhids capture Baghdad and end Abbasid power

A.D. 1000
999–1030 Mahmud of Ghazni, an Afghan Muslim, invades northwest India

1038 Seljuk Turks from central Asia conquer Persia

1055 Seljuk Turks take Baghdad and become major force in Islamic world

A.D. 1100

The Arab world:
Islamic culture

In the centuries following the death of Muhammad and the Arab invasion of the Middle East, North Africa, and Spain, Muslim scientists, scholars, and engineers developed a culture that was unrivaled in the world at that time. They made huge advances in astronomy, medicine, and mathematics—giving the world algebra, trigonometry, and the decimal fraction—and translated many earlier Greek and Indian works into their own language, Arabic. They also developed a highly decorative architecture that made great use of landscape design and calligraphy (decorative writing).

Art and calligraphy

The Islamic faith discourages the depiction of Allah (God) and Muhammad. If Muslim artists do show Muhammad in books or paintings, they always cover his face with a veil. They also use beautiful calligraphy to write out and decorate the verses of the Koran, their holy book, as this 16th-century example shows.

Astronomy

Muslim scholars were world leaders in astronomy, and most major Muslim cities had at least one observatory. Muslim astronomers also developed the astrolabe (left). This is a device that was used by navigators to measure the height of the sun at noon so that they could work out their latitude—how far north or south they were.

Medicine

This Islamic painting shows a doctor visiting a patient. The most important Muslim physician was Ibn Sina (980–1037), a Persian scholar who wrote the 14-volume *Canon of Medicine*, which later formed the basis of European medicine until the 1600s. Muslims disapproved of surgery, but they did use it when necessary and were the first people to remove cataracts to restore eyesight.

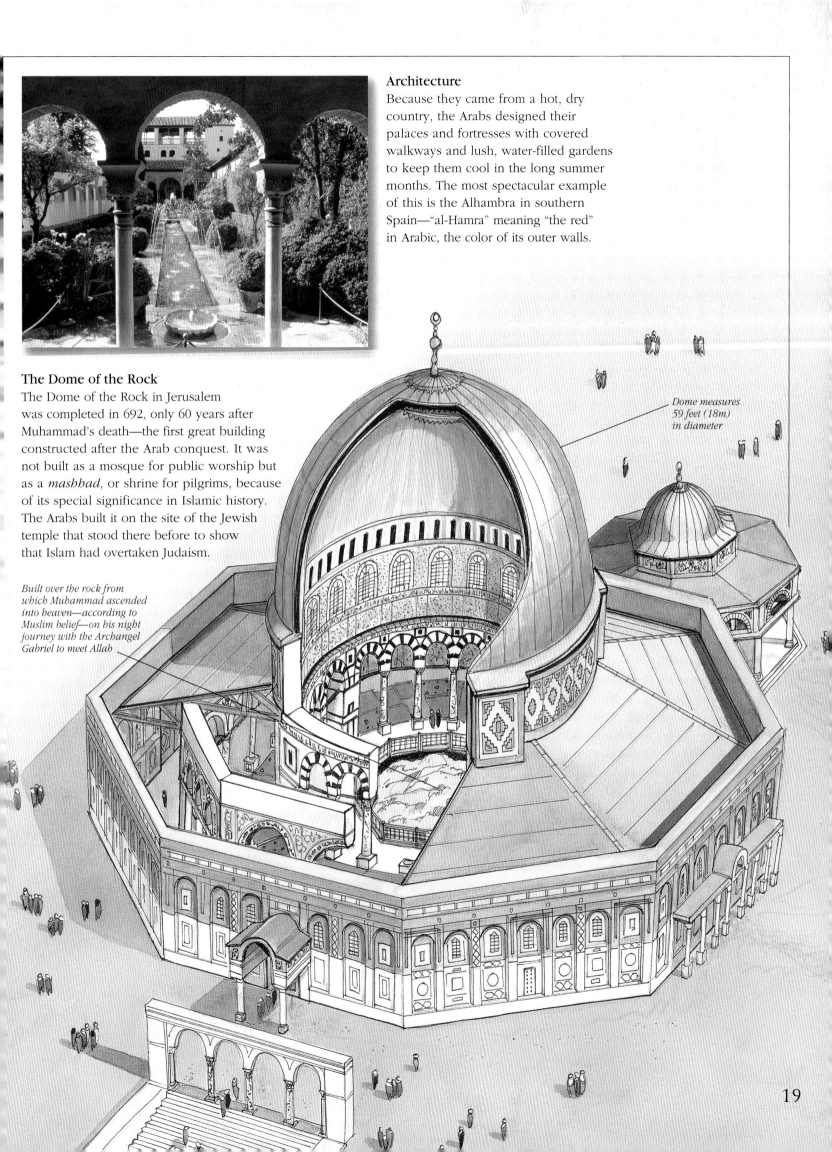

Architecture

Because they came from a hot, dry country, the Arabs designed their palaces and fortresses with covered walkways and lush, water-filled gardens to keep them cool in the long summer months. The most spectacular example of this is the Alhambra in southern Spain—"al-Hamra" meaning "the red" in Arabic, the color of its outer walls.

The Dome of the Rock

The Dome of the Rock in Jerusalem was completed in 692, only 60 years after Muhammad's death—the first great building constructed after the Arab conquest. It was not built as a mosque for public worship but as a *mashhad*, or shrine for pilgrims, because of its special significance in Islamic history. The Arabs built it on the site of the Jewish temple that stood there before to show that Islam had overtaken Judaism.

Dome measures 59 feet (18m) in diameter

Built over the rock from which Muhammad ascended into heaven—according to Muslim belief—on his night journey with the Archangel Gabriel to meet Allah

19

Medieval India

The Hindu and Buddhist dominance of India came to an end in A.D. 711, when Arab armies brought Islam across the Indus river into western India. From then on, Muslims (followers of Islam) and Hindus waged a constant battle to control the Indian subcontinent. In 1175, in what is now Afghanistan, Muhammad of Ghur and his army broke through into the Ganges river valley in the north. This paved the way for more than 600 years of Muslim domination in India. After Muhammad's death in 1206, one of his most trusted generals, Qutb-ud-Din, established the independent Sultanate of Delhi. This sultanate controlled everything except the southern tip of the country by 1351.

Raiding party
The war-hungry Muslim ruler Mahmud of Ghazni launched 17 invasions of India after the year 999, raiding and destroying Hindu temples.

Ghur

Ghazni

Timur
In 1398 Timur the Lame, a Turkish nomad from central Asia, invaded India and ransacked Delhi.

Indus

Mult

Sind

Islam
Arab Muslims conquered Sind in 711, introducing Islam to the subcontinent. The new religion slowly spread east and south across India.

Making pots

Gujarat

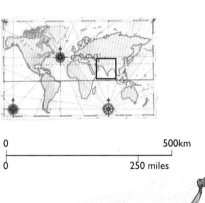

0   500km
0   250 miles

Inshore fishing

Arabian Sea

Hinduism

Although Muslims ruled much of India during this period, most people remained Hindu, with some keeping their Buddhist or Jain faith. Hindu kingdoms flourished in the south and east of the country, the Cholas of southern India even exporting Hinduism throughout southeast Asia. This picture shows the 11th-century Brahmeswar Siva temple at Bhubaneswar, in eastern India. Hindu temples of this kind were incredibly wealthy, with large estates of land and donations from wealthy people eager to please the gods.

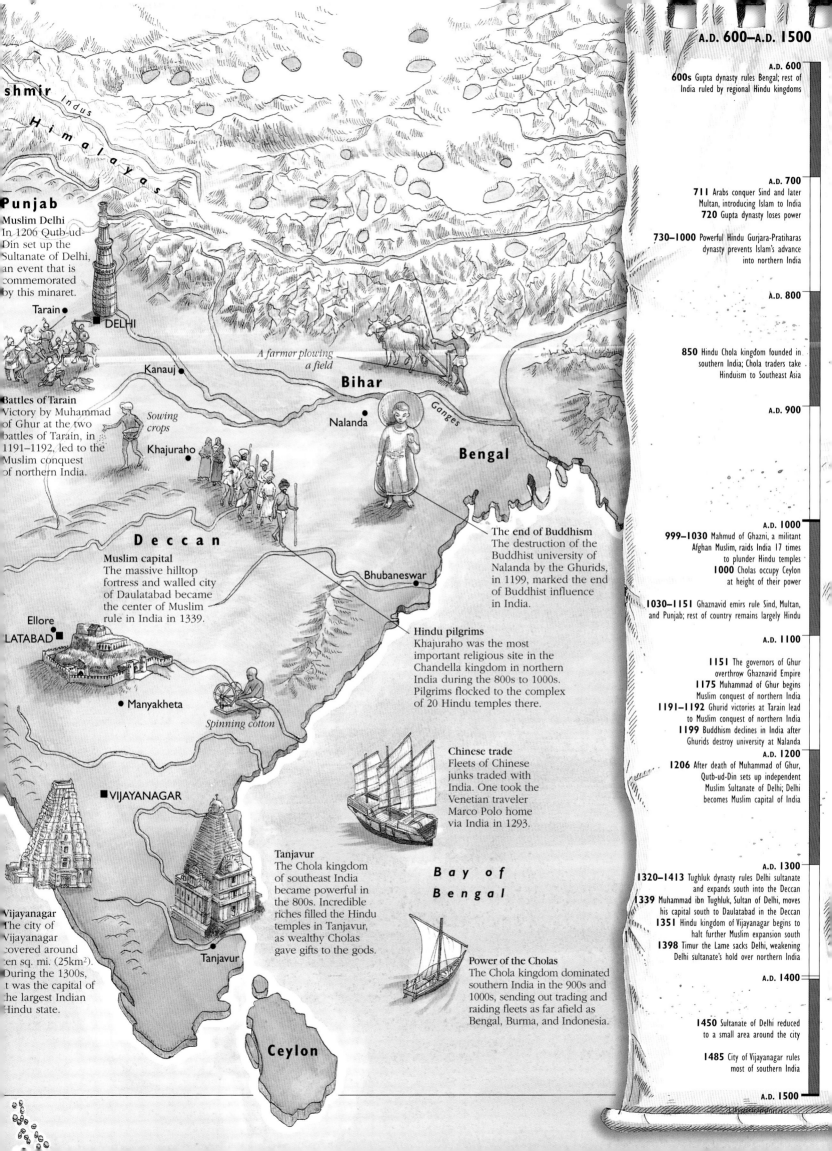

shmir _Indus_

H i m a l a y a s

Punjab

Muslim Delhi
In 1206 Qutb-ud-Din set up the Sultanate of Delhi, an event that is commemorated by this minaret.

Tarain •
■ DELHI

Battles of Tarain
Victory by Muhammad of Ghur at the two battles of Tarain, in 1191–1192, led to the Muslim conquest of northern India.

Kanauj •

Sowing crops

Khajuraho •

A farmer plowing a field

Bihar

Nalanda •

Ganges

Bengal

D e c c a n

Muslim capital
The massive hilltop fortress and walled city of Daulatabad became the center of Muslim rule in India in 1339.

Ellore •
LATABAD ■

The end of Buddhism
The destruction of the Buddhist university of Nalanda by the Ghurids, in 1199, marked the end of Buddhist influence in India.

Bhubaneswar •

Hindu pilgrims
Khajuraho was the most important religious site in the Chandella kingdom in northern India during the 800s to 1000s. Pilgrims flocked to the complex of 20 Hindu temples there.

• Manyakheta

Spinning cotton

Chinese trade
Fleets of Chinese junks traded with India. One took the Venetian traveler Marco Polo home via India in 1293.

■ VIJAYANAGAR

Tanjavur
The Chola kingdom of southeast India became powerful in the 800s. Incredible riches filled the Hindu temples in Tanjavur, as wealthy Cholas gave gifts to the gods.

**B a y   o f
B e n g a l**

Vijayanagar
The city of Vijayanagar covered around ten sq. mi. (25km²). During the 1300s, it was the capital of the largest Indian Hindu state.

Tanjavur •

Power of the Cholas
The Chola kingdom dominated southern India in the 900s and 1000s, sending out trading and raiding fleets as far afield as Bengal, Burma, and Indonesia.

Ceylon

A.D. 600—A.D. 1500

A.D. 600
600s Gupta dynasty rules Bengal; rest of India ruled by regional Hindu kingdoms

A.D. 700
711 Arabs conquer Sind and later Multan, introducing Islam to India
720 Gupta dynasty loses power

730–1000 Powerful Hindu Gurjara-Pratiharas dynasty prevents Islam's advance into northern India

A.D. 800

850 Hindu Chola kingdom founded in southern India; Chola traders take Hinduism to Southeast Asia

A.D. 900

A.D. 1000
999–1030 Mahmud of Ghazni, a militant Afghan Muslim, raids India 17 times to plunder Hindu temples
1000 Cholas occupy Ceylon at height of their power

1030–1151 Ghaznavid emirs rule Sind, Multan, and Punjab; rest of country remains largely Hindu

A.D. 1100

1151 The governors of Ghur overthrow Ghaznavid Empire
1175 Muhammad of Ghur begins Muslim conquest of northern India
1191–1192 Ghurid victories at Tarain lead to Muslim conquest of northern India
1199 Buddhism declines in India after Ghurids destroy university at Nalanda

A.D. 1200
1206 After death of Muhammad of Ghur, Qutb-ud-Din sets up independent Muslim Sultanate of Delhi; Delhi becomes Muslim capital of India

A.D. 1300
1320–1413 Tughluk dynasty rules Delhi sultanate and expands south into the Deccan
1339 Muhammad ibn Tughluk, Sultan of Delhi, moves his capital south to Daulatabad in the Deccan
1351 Hindu kingdom of Vijayanagar begins to halt further Muslim expansion south
1398 Timur the Lame sacks Delhi, weakening Delhi sultanate's hold over northern India

A.D. 1400

1450 Sultanate of Delhi reduced to a small area around the city

1485 City of Vijayanagar rules most of southern India

A.D. 1500

Battle of the Talas river
In 751 China's expansion into central Asia was stopped by an Arab army at the Talas river. From then on, the peoples of this region became Muslim.

Gunpowder
The Chinese first used gunpowder in warfare in around 850. By 969 they were using it to fire rockets at their enemies.

Altai Mountains

Tian Shan Mountains

Tingzhou

Kucha

Turfan

Karashahr

Kashgar

Taklimakan Desert

Gansu Corridor

Qilian Mountains

Hotan

Gilgit

The Silk Road
Caravans of camels bearing silk and other goods headed west along the Silk Road, an ancient trading route connecting China with western lands.

Frontier forts
The Chinese built forts around the Taklimakan Desert in the 650s to protect their western frontier from attacks.

Buddhist learning
The Buddhist monk Xuan Zang left for India in 629. He returned 16 years later with Buddhist texts that he had translated from Sanskrit.

these lines show the various routes taken along the Silk Road

TIBET

Himalayas

China

Since the end of the Han dynasty in A.D. 220, China had been divided among three warring kingdoms. In 589 Yang Jian reunited the country by force, and as Emperor Wen, established the short-lived Sui dynasty. The succeeding Tang dynasty, which ruled from 618 to 907, introduced strong government and presided over great achievements in technology and the arts, especially poetry. The collapse of the Tang dynasty saw China fall apart again during the "Ten Kingdoms and Five Dynasties" period, but in 960 the country was reunited by the Song dynasty. The Song were the most effective governors in Chinese history, and under their rule, China became rich and its people grew prosperous.

Printing
During the 700s, the Chinese perfected the technique of printing words and pictures onto paper using engraved blocks of wood. This enabled them to print multiple copies of banknotes, documents, and then whole books. An example is the *Diamond Sutra* (above), the world's first printed book, which dates from 868. At first the printers had to engrave whole pages onto the blocks—but in around the year 1000 they invented "movable type," allowing them to set individual earthenware letters to make up words and sentences.

Invasion from the north
In 1127 the Jurchen from Manchuria seized much of northern China, keeping control until the Mongols conquered their empire 100 years later.

Gobi Desert

Traders bringing furs from the north

The Great Wall
The Great Wall was regularly strengthened to keep out invaders from the north—but it did not always succeed in doing so!

Beijing

Fields being irrigated

KOREA

The Grand Canal
In the early 600s the Chinese built a massive internal waterway, linking Yue to Beijing via Luoyang.

Barges carrying grain and other products to Changan

Yellow River   Kaifeng
CHANGAN   Luoyang

Changan
The Tang capital of Changan had more than one million inhabitants in ?50. It was the world's biggest city at that time.

Granaries
Wen, the first Sui emperor, had granaries built to store grain—in case of a food shortage.

Yangtze

Growing rice

Yue
Hangzhou

Government
Taizong, the second Tang emperor, created a strong, central administration and introduced a tough entrance exam for new public servants.

CHINA

Oxen being used to plow fields

Porcelain
The first true porcelain was made in eastern China during the Tang period. In the west we call this pottery "china."

Tea
Buddhist monks brought tea bushes into China from the lower slopes of the Himalayas in India. Tea soon became a national drink.

Printing block for making books and documents

Guangzhou

Typical Chinese house

Death of an emperor
The last Song emperor drowned in a naval battle with the Mongols off the island of Yashan, near Guangzhou, in 1279.

600km
300 miles

A.D. 500

589 General Yang Jian reunites China, and as Emperor Wen, founds Sui dynasty

A.D. 600

604–617 Wen's successor, Yang, tries to conquer Korea and fails; peasants revolt against him
606–609 Grand Canal is constructed
617 Li Yuan captures Sui capital of Luoyang
618 Li Yuan becomes first Tang emperor, as Gaozu
626 Gaozu deposed (removed from power) by his son Taizong, one of China's most capable rulers

640–659 Chinese expand into central Asia

A.D. 700

700s Block printing is invented

751 Arab victory over Chinese at Talas river ends Chinese control of central Asia

791 Tibetans seize western China after their military victory at Tingzhou

A.D. 800

825 Chamber locks first installed on Chinese canals

c. 850 Gunpowder first used in warfare

859–884 Peasant revolts weaken Tang government

A.D. 900

907 Tang Empire collapses
907–960 China divided between the Five Dynasties state and the Ten Kingdoms

960 Song Taizu becomes emperor of the Five Dynasties and begins reuniting China
979 Song Taizu's brother Song Taizong reunites China and founds Song dynasty; start of Northern Song period

A.D. 1000

c. 1000 Printing by movable type invented

1090 Water-driven mechanical clock constructed for Song court

A.D. 1100

1117–1124 Jurchen people of Manchuria conquer Liao state north of China and set up Jin Empire
1127 Jin invade and capture Song capital of Kaifeng; Song retreat south and establish new capital at Hangzhou— start of Southern Song period

1150 Chinese navigators begin using magnetic compass

A.D. 1200

1200 Chinese build ships with watertight bulkheads to make them safer at sea
1200 Water-powered textile machinery first used
1226 Mongols overrun western China
1234 Mongols conquer northern China and begin attacking the Southern Song Empire

1279 Mongols conquer Southern Song Empire

A.D. 1300

Japan and Korea

The histories of Korea and Japan are both entangled with that of their powerful neighbor, China. The Korean kingdom of Silla managed to throw the Chinese off the Korean peninsula in A.D. 676 and eventually unify the country under the ruling Koryo dynasty by 936. Both Korea and Japan tried to create strong, centralized states—as China had done—but in Japan powerful families undermined the authority of the emperor. One such family, the Fujiwaras, effectively became the rulers of the country in 858. However, as the emperor withdrew from public life, rival warlords and samurai (warrior knights) fought each other for control.

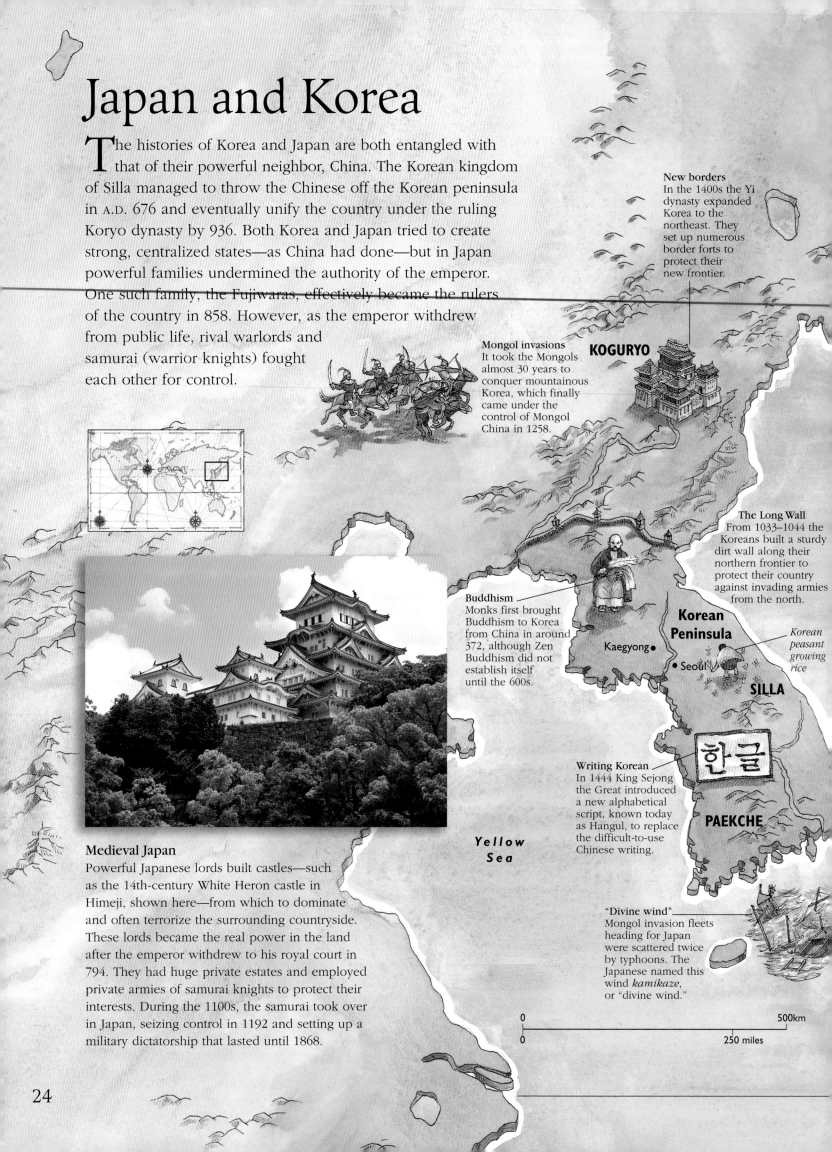

New borders
In the 1400s the Yi dynasty expanded Korea to the northeast. They set up numerous border forts to protect their new frontier.

Mongol invasions
It took the Mongols almost 30 years to conquer mountainous Korea, which finally came under the control of Mongol China in 1258.

KOGURYO

The Long Wall
From 1033–1044 the Koreans built a sturdy dirt wall along their northern frontier to protect their country against invading armies from the north.

Buddhism
Monks first brought Buddhism to Korea from China in around 372, although Zen Buddhism did not establish itself until the 600s.

Korean Peninsula

Kaegyong

Seoul

Korean peasant growing rice

SILLA

한글

Writing Korean
In 1444 King Sejong the Great introduced a new alphabetical script, known today as Hangul, to replace the difficult-to-use Chinese writing.

PAEKCHE

Yellow Sea

Medieval Japan
Powerful Japanese lords built castles—such as the 14th-century White Heron castle in Himeji, shown here—from which to dominate and often terrorize the surrounding countryside. These lords became the real power in the land after the emperor withdrew to his royal court in 794. They had huge private estates and employed private armies of samurai knights to protect their interests. During the 1100s, the samurai took over in Japan, seizing control in 1192 and setting up a military dictatorship that lasted until 1868.

"Divine wind"
Mongol invasion fleets heading for Japan were scattered twice by typhoons. The Japanese named this wind *kamikaze*, or "divine wind."

0 ——————————— 500km
0 ——————————— 250 miles

Independent islanders
Primitive hunter-gatherers, unrelated to the Japanese, lived on the northern island of Hokkaido, which did not become part of Japan until the 1600s.

Hokkaido

Pacific Ocean

Trade links
Trade, cultural, and religious links between China, Korea, and Japan were common, but smugglers and pirates tried to evade customs fees and other restrictions.

Sea of Japan

Wooden houses
Japanese houses were built of light wood so that they could easily be restored or rebuilt if they were damaged by an earthquake.

Inshore fishing around Japan

Growing rice in Japan

Tale of Genji
Lady Murasaki Shikibu wrote the epic *Tale of Genji*, one of the world's first novels, at the royal court in 1007.

Coming of spring
During the 700s, the emperor decreed that people should celebrate the arrival of cherry blossoms in the spring.

Honshu

J A P A N

End of the Taira
Samurai warriors from the Taira clan were defeated at the battle of Dannoura in 1185.

Mount Fuji
Mount Fuji, known locally as Fuji san, is the sacred mountain of Japan.

• Heian

• Himeji

■ NARA

Nara
In 710 the Japanese established their first capital in Nara, later an important center for the Buddhist religion.

• Dannoura

Shikoku

• Hakata Bay

Kyushu

White Heron castle
Local warlords built large stone castles such as the White Heron castle in Himeji. They commanded their estates from these castles.

No theater
In the 1300s Kan'ami Kiyotsugo developed a formal style of drama known as No theater, in which actors use expressive masks.

Whale hunting
Whales have always been an important source of food for the Japanese.

A.D. 500
500s Koguryo, Silla, and Paekche kingdoms emerge in Korea

552 Buddhism introduced into Japan from Korea
562 Japanese expelled from Korea after 200 years of occupation

A.D. 600
604 Prince Shotoku introduces Chinese-style government, giving power to the Japanese emperor instead of to the nobility
646 New Taika reforms bring all Japanese land into imperial ownership
660–676 Chinese occupy most of Korea until driven out by Silla

A.D. 700
700s Japanese Shinto religion merges with Buddhism
708 First official coins minted in Japan
710 Japanese capital set up in Nara
780 Struggle between king and powerful lords leads to breakup of Silla
794 Emperor Kammu moves Japanese royal court to Heian (modern-day Kyoto) and gives land to the nobility

A.D. 800

858 Fujiwara Yorifusa becomes regent of Japan; his family now runs Japan

A.D. 900

918–936 Koryo dynasty unifies Silla and unites Korea for the first time

A.D. 1000
1007 Lady Murasaki Shikibu writes *Tale of Genji* at the royal court in Heian

1033–1044 Koreans build the Long Wall to protect their country from northern enemies

A.D. 1100
1100s Fujiwaras lose power to armed samurai clans

1180–1185 Gempei war in Japan between Taira and Minamoto samurai clans ends in Taira defeat
1192 Minamoto Yoritomo establishes military shogunate government in Japan

A.D. 1200

1231–1258 Mongols subdue Korea, which then falls under control of Mongol China

1274, 1281 Kublai Khan's two attempts to invade Japan from Korea are both destroyed by *kamikaze* ("divine wind") typhoons

A.D. 1300
1333–1336 Go-Daigo tries but fails to restore direct imperial rule in Japan
1356 End of Mongol rule in Korea

1392 Yi dynasty takes power in Korea (until 1910) and expands country to its borders of today

A.D. 1400

1444 King Sejong the Great of Korea introduces the new alphabetical Hangul script

1467–1477 Civil war between rival samurai clans in Japan

A.D. 1500

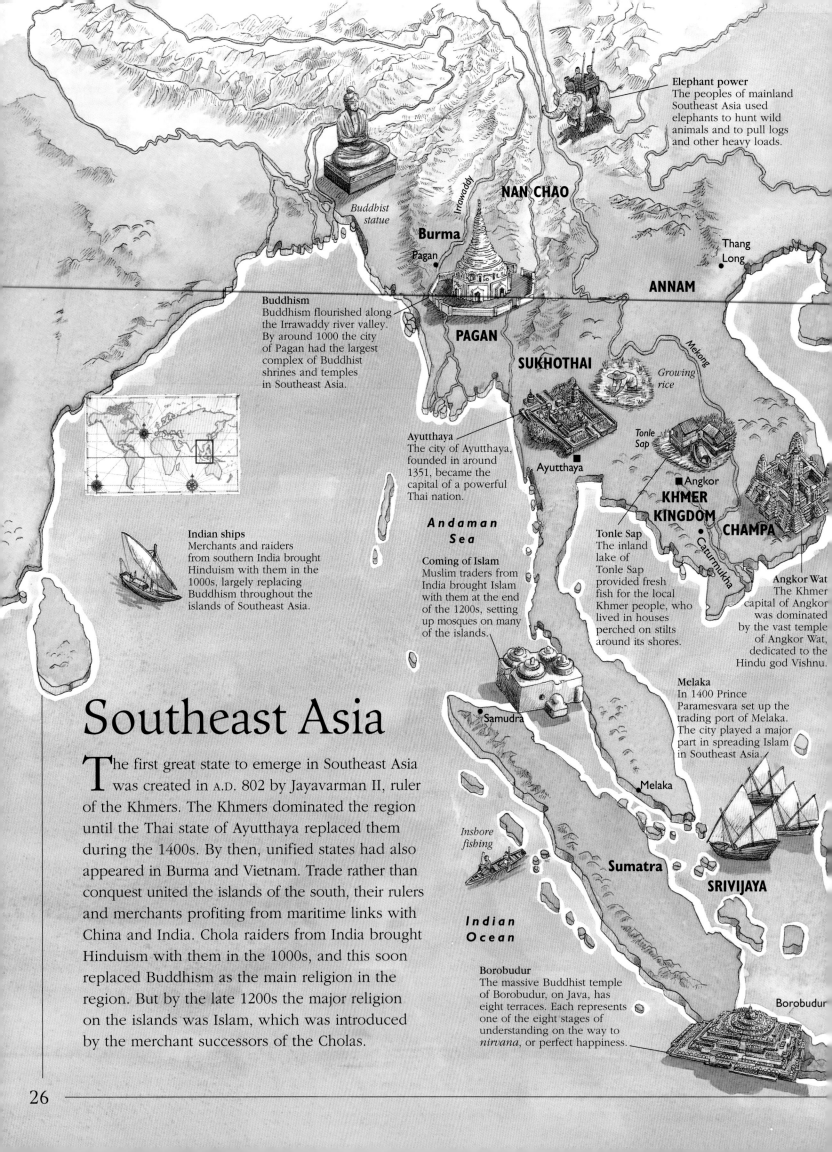

Elephant power
The peoples of mainland Southeast Asia used elephants to hunt wild animals and to pull logs and other heavy loads.

Buddhist statue

NAN CHAO

Irrawaddy

Burma
Pagan

Thang Long

ANNAM

Buddhism
Buddhism flourished along the Irrawaddy river valley. By around 1000 the city of Pagan had the largest complex of Buddhist shrines and temples in Southeast Asia.

PAGAN

SUKHOTHAI

Mekong

Growing rice

Tonle Sap

Ayutthaya
The city of Ayutthaya, founded in around 1351, became the capital of a powerful Thai nation.

Ayutthaya

Angkor

KHMER KINGDOM

CHAMPA

Caturmukha

Indian ships
Merchants and raiders from southern India brought Hinduism with them in the 1000s, largely replacing Buddhism throughout the islands of Southeast Asia.

Andaman Sea

Coming of Islam
Muslim traders from India brought Islam with them at the end of the 1200s, setting up mosques on many of the islands.

Tonle Sap
The inland lake of Tonle Sap provided fresh fish for the local Khmer people, who lived in houses perched on stilts around its shores.

Angkor Wat
The Khmer capital of Angkor was dominated by the vast temple of Angkor Wat, dedicated to the Hindu god Vishnu.

Melaka
In 1400 Prince Paramesvara set up the trading port of Melaka. The city played a major part in spreading Islam in Southeast Asia.

Samudra

Melaka

Southeast Asia

The first great state to emerge in Southeast Asia was created in A.D. 802 by Jayavarman II, ruler of the Khmers. The Khmers dominated the region until the Thai state of Ayutthaya replaced them during the 1400s. By then, unified states had also appeared in Burma and Vietnam. Trade rather than conquest united the islands of the south, their rulers and merchants profiting from maritime links with China and India. Chola raiders from India brought Hinduism with them in the 1000s, and this soon replaced Buddhism as the main religion in the region. But by the late 1200s the major religion on the islands was Islam, which was introduced by the merchant successors of the Cholas.

Inshore fishing

Sumatra

SRIVIJAYA

Indian Ocean

Borobudur
The massive Buddhist temple of Borobudur, on Java, has eight terraces. Each represents one of the eight stages of understanding on the way to *nirvana*, or perfect happiness.

Borobudur

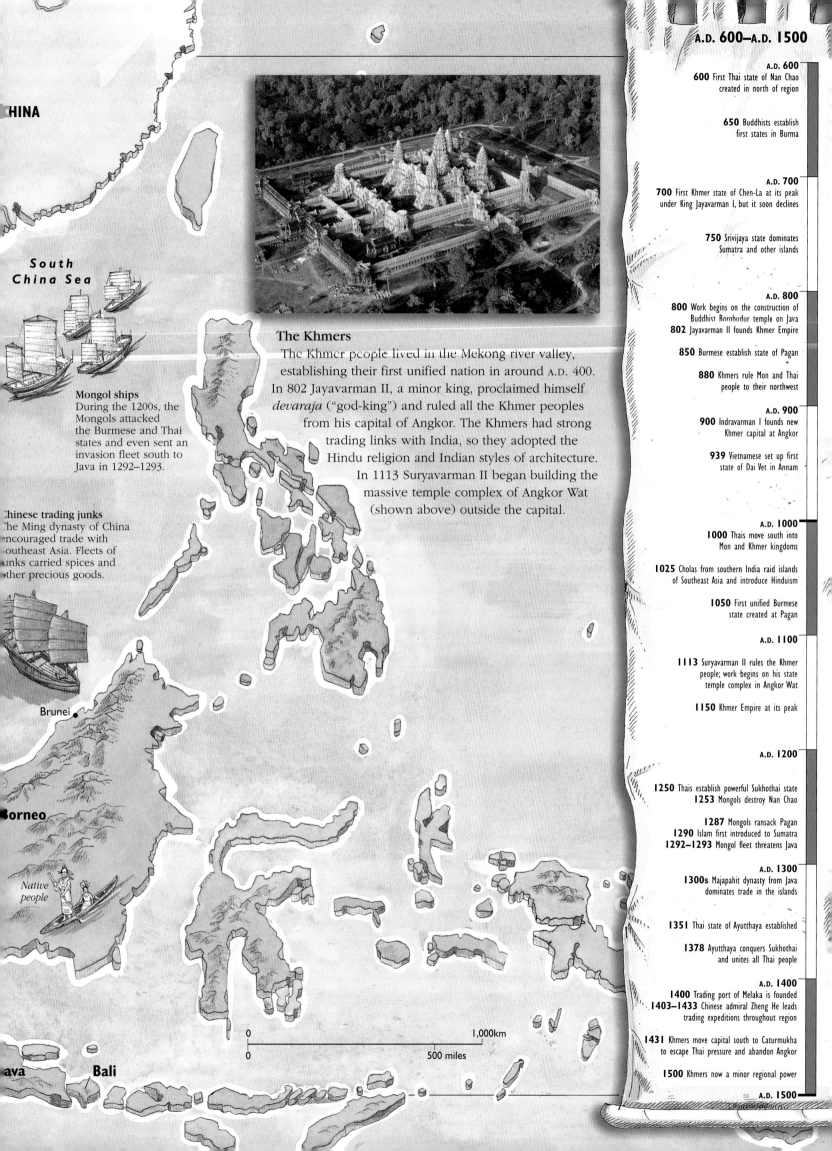

CHINA

South
China Sea

Mongol ships
During the 1200s, the
Mongols attacked
the Burmese and Thai
states and even sent an
invasion fleet south to
Java in 1292–1293.

Chinese trading junks
The Ming dynasty of China
encouraged trade with
Southeast Asia. Fleets of
junks carried spices and
other precious goods.

Brunei

Borneo

*Native
people*

Java   **Bali**

0   1,000km

0   500 miles

The Khmers

The Khmer people lived in the Mekong river valley,
establishing their first unified nation in around A.D. 400.
In 802 Jayavarman II, a minor king, proclaimed himself
devaraja ("god-king") and ruled all the Khmer peoples
from his capital of Angkor. The Khmers had strong
trading links with India, so they adopted the
Hindu religion and Indian styles of architecture.
In 1113 Suryavarman II began building the
massive temple complex of Angkor Wat
(shown above) outside the capital.

A.D. 600
600 First Thai state of Nan Chao
created in north of region

650 Buddhists establish
first states in Burma

A.D. 700
700 First Khmer state of Chen-La at its peak
under King Jayavarman I, but it soon declines

750 Srivijaya state dominates
Sumatra and other islands

A.D. 800
800 Work begins on the construction of
Buddhist Borobudur temple on Java
802 Jayavarman II founds Khmer Empire

850 Burmese establish state of Pagan

880 Khmers rule Mon and Thai
people to their northwest

A.D. 900
900 Indravarman I founds new
Khmer capital at Angkor

939 Vietnamese set up first
state of Dai Vet in Annam

A.D. 1000
1000 Thais move south into
Mon and Khmer kingdoms

1025 Cholas from southern India raid islands
of Southeast Asia and introduce Hinduism

1050 First unified Burmese
state created at Pagan

A.D. 1100

1113 Suryavarman II rules the Khmer
people; work begins on his state
temple complex in Angkor Wat

1150 Khmer Empire at its peak

A.D. 1200

1250 Thais establish powerful Sukhothai state
1253 Mongols destroy Nan Chao

1287 Mongols ransack Pagan
1290 Islam first introduced to Sumatra
1292–1293 Mongol fleet threatens Java

A.D. 1300
1300s Majapahit dynasty from Java
dominates trade in the islands

1351 Thai state of Ayutthaya established

1378 Ayutthaya conquers Sukhothai
and unites all Thai people

A.D. 1400
1400 Trading port of Melaka is founded
1403–1433 Chinese admiral Zheng He leads
trading expeditions throughout region

1431 Khmers move capital south to Caturmukha
to escape Thai pressure and abandon Angkor

1500 Khmers now a minor regional power

A.D. 1500

The Pacific

For more than 1,000 years, intrepid Polynesian navigators from Tahiti, and elsewhere in the central Pacific Ocean, had sailed out to colonize the more remote islands. By around A.D. 1000 they had reached Aotearoa, which we now call New Zealand. Its two large islands were far colder and wetter than their homelands farther north, and they had to learn to cultivate new crops and build better shelters. They hunted the moa, a large flightless bird, for its meat and grew sweet potatoes and other crops. On many of the Pacific islands, the Polynesians built ceremonial platforms out of coral, called *marae*, where their priests conducted religious and social ceremonies.

Hawaii

Heiau
The *heiau* of Hawaii are very similar to the *marae* found on other Polynesian islands. They had raised platforms on which the priests stood to conduct religious ceremonies.

South Pacific Ocean

Line Islands

Basket weaving
Women wove baskets, bowls, and other items from the leaves of the coconut palm.

Atoll fishing
Throughout the region, Polynesians caught fish by standing on the semisubmerged coral atolls and attacking fish with spears.

Tuvalu

Society Islands

Samoa

Thatched home

Fiji

Cook Islands

Tonga

Musical instruments

Fishing equipment
Fishermen carved pearl shells to make hooks. They twisted coconut fibers to create lines and nets.

Hillside terraces
On hilly islands, such as Hawaii and the Cook Islands, farmers built terraces on the steep hillsides in which to grow crops such as taro and other root vegetables.

Kermadec

Tasman Sea

Inshore fishing
Fishermen caught their fish from a simple canoe stabilized by a special frame called an outrigger.

Sails being made from palm leaves.

Combat
Maori warriors fought each other with spears or clubs made of whalebone or greenstone, a type of jade.

Maori tattoos
A Maori chief, or *rangatiri*, had his face tattooed as a mark of his importance. His clothes were made out of flax and kiwi feathers.

Oceangoing canoe
The Polynesians traveled thousands of miles in twin-hulled canoes. These canoes could carry up to 200 people as well as all their supplies for the long voyage.

Maori warrior hunting a moa

Aotearoa

Chatham Islands

A.D. 500
by 500 Polynesians have reached the Hawaiian Islands, their most northerly settlement in the Pacific

A.D. 600
600 Ceremonial *marae*, or platforms, common throughout the Pacific islands

A.D. 700
700 Easter Islanders begin to build ceremonial *ahu*, or platforms

A.D. 800

A.D. 900
c. 900 Polynesians settle in remote Pitcairn Islands

A.D. 1000
c. 1000 Polynesians begin settling in Aotearoa (New Zealand)
1000 Easter Islanders begin carving giant statues
1050 South American sweet potato grown on Cook Islands, suggesting contact between Polynesians and Native Americans

A.D. 1100
1100 Polynesians reach Chatham Islands, their last settlement in the Pacific

A.D. 1200
1200 Tribal chiefdoms develop throughout Polynesia

A.D. 1300
1300 Conflict between rival Maori tribes leads to construction of *pas* (fortified settlements) in Aotearoa

A.D. 1400

A.D. 1500

Easter Island

Polynesian navigators reached the remote Easter Island in the eastern Pacific in around A.D. 300. In around A.D. 1000 the 7,000 or so inhabitants of the island began to carve huge stone statues in the island's three main quarries. They used hammers made out of basalt rock because they had no iron. Once they were finished, the Polynesians hauled these massive statues across the island on wooden sleds, using palm trunks as levers and rollers to help them, and erected the statues on platforms in their ceremonial *ahu*—the equivalent of the *marae* platforms that were found elsewhere in the Pacific.

Leaf plates
Polynesians lived off seafood, yams, and fruits, eating their food from plates made of leaves.

Marquesas Islands

Marae
A *marae* was used for religious and ceremonial purposes. It consisted of a flat court paved with coral and a series of raised platforms. Upright slabs marked where the priests and officials stood.

Tahiti

Rope being made from coconut palm fibers

Pitcairn Islands

Outrigger canoe

Island statues
Easter Islanders carved and erected more than 1,000 stone statues—probably to honor their ancestors. Some of these statues had inlaid eyes of white coral and red obsidian, a dark volcanic glass.

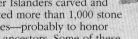

Easter Island

South Pacific Ocean

Humpback whale

0 — 2,000km
0 — 1,000 miles

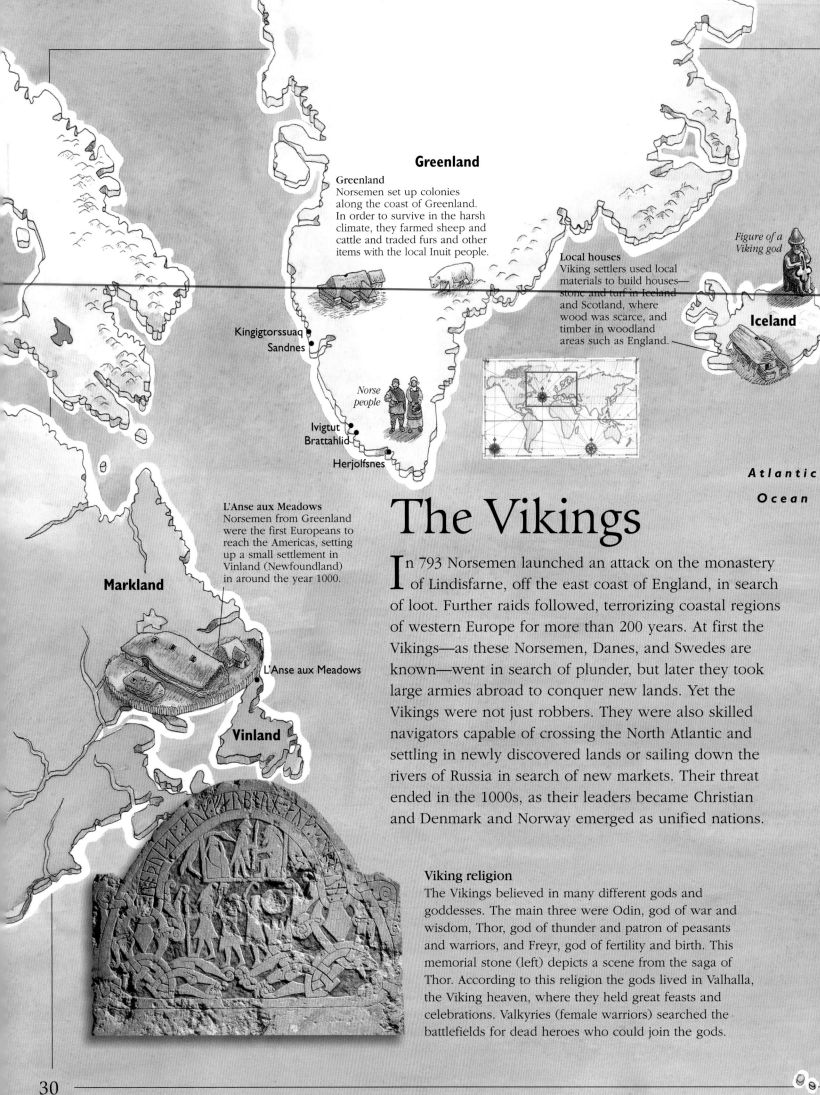

Greenland

Greenland
Norsemen set up colonies along the coast of Greenland. In order to survive in the harsh climate, they farmed sheep and cattle and traded furs and other items with the local Inuit people.

Figure of a Viking god

Local houses
Viking settlers used local materials to build houses—stone and turf in Iceland and Scotland, where wood was scarce, and timber in woodland areas such as England.

Iceland

Kingigtorssuaq
Sandnes

Norse people

Ivigtut
Brattahlid

Herjolfsnes

L'Anse aux Meadows
Norsemen from Greenland were the first Europeans to reach the Americas, setting up a small settlement in Vinland (Newfoundland) in around the year 1000.

Markland

L'Anse aux Meadows

Vinland

Atlantic Ocean

The Vikings

In 793 Norsemen launched an attack on the monastery of Lindisfarne, off the east coast of England, in search of loot. Further raids followed, terrorizing coastal regions of western Europe for more than 200 years. At first the Vikings—as these Norsemen, Danes, and Swedes are known—went in search of plunder, but later they took large armies abroad to conquer new lands. Yet the Vikings were not just robbers. They were also skilled navigators capable of crossing the North Atlantic and settling in newly discovered lands or sailing down the rivers of Russia in search of new markets. Their threat ended in the 1000s, as their leaders became Christian and Denmark and Norway emerged as unified nations.

Viking religion
The Vikings believed in many different gods and goddesses. The main three were Odin, god of war and wisdom, Thor, god of thunder and patron of peasants and warriors, and Freyr, god of fertility and birth. This memorial stone (left) depicts a scene from the saga of Thor. According to this religion the gods lived in Valhalla, the Viking heaven, where they held great feasts and celebrations. Valkyries (female warriors) searched the battlefields for dead heroes who could join the gods.

Rune stones
The Vikings celebrated battles and heroes by erecting stones that were carved with pictures and words in their runic alphabet.

Funeral ships
Viking chieftains were buried in their ships with all they would need for the afterlife. Some ships were covered with mounds of dirt while others were set on fire.

Sailing to Iceland
Between 870 and 930, more than 10,000 Norsemen made the seven-day crossing of the North Atlantic to settle in Iceland.

Viking log home

Longhorn cow

Woolly sheep

Norway

Sweden

Gotland
Paviken in Gotland was the major Viking commercial center in the Baltic, trading amber and furs for silks, spices, and silver from as far away as Constantinople and Baghdad.

Novgorod

Lindisfarne monastery raided by Vikings

Gotland

Silver brooch

Denmark

Baltic Sea

Smolensk

Rus traders
Swedish traders sailed down the Dnieper and Volga rivers to the Black and Caspian seas. The locals called these Vikings "Rus."

Viking forts
During the 980s, King Harald Bluetooth built four huge circular forts in Denmark.

Lindisfarne

cotland

York

England

Dublin

North Sea

Wessex

Danelaw

Hamburg

Rhine

Louvain

Viking trade
Vikings erected rune stones along their trade routes, which covered a wide area. Arab silver coins have been found in Sweden.

Kiev

CAROLINGIAN EMPIRE

Rouen

Nantes

Loire

Normans
n 911 the rench king llowed Danes o settle around ouen in France.

Viking warriors

Arles

Pisa

Narbonne

antiago de Compostela

KINGDOM OF THE TURIAS AND LEÓN

UMAYYAD EMIRATE

Viking sword

Black Sea

BYZANTINE EMPIRE

Constantinople

Seville

Plunder
Vikings raided Mediterranean ports for loot, sailing up the rivers to attack inland towns.

Mediterranean Sea

IDRISID CALIPHATE

North Africa

0 ——— 1,000km
0 ——— 500 miles

A.D. 700

A.D. 750

793 Norse raiders attack Lindisfarne monastery on coast of England, the first of many raids against the British Isles
799 First Norse raids on Frankish coast; Charlemagne sets up coastal defenses to protect his empire

A.D. 800

830s Start of large-scale raids against British Isles and Carolingian Empire

841 Norsemen establish a trading base in Dublin
845 The Franks buy off the raiders by paying them Danegeld (protection money)

A.D. 850
859–862 Viking raiders attack Mediterranean ports
862 Rus create first Russian state around Novgorod
865 Danish Great Army invades England
870 Norsemen settle in Iceland

878 Alfred, King of Wessex, defeats Danes and restricts them to the eastern Danelaw region of Britain

A.D. 900

911 Charles the Simple of France allows Danes to settle around Rouen, leading to the creation of Normandy

A.D. 950
954 Viking kingdom of York falls to English king

965 Harald Bluetooth of Denmark is first Viking king to be baptized a Christian

980 Danes renew their raids on England
986 Erik the Red founds Norse settlements in Greenland

A.D. 1000
1000 Norse settlement established at L'Anse aux Meadows on North American coast

1014 Danes conquer England
1016–1035 King Canute rules vast kingdom of Denmark, Norway, and England

A.D. 1050

1066 The Normans (the Danes that settled in Normandy) conquer England

A.D. 1100

Medieval Europe

Medieval Europe was dominated by two great institutions: the feudal system and the Catholic Church. Feudalism began in France during the A.D. 700s and eventually spread throughout Europe. Kings granted estates to their leading noblemen in return for military service. Knights fought for these noblemen and received smaller estates of land, farmed by serfs (peasants) in return for military protection. This structure was bound together by oaths of loyalty. The Catholic Church was the sole religious authority in western Europe but also claimed increasing control over secular (nonreligious) rulers, leading to constant struggles with powerful emperors and kings.

The Crusades

In 1095 Pope Urban II (right, above throne) issued a call to European leaders to win back the Holy Land from Muslim control because the Seljuk Turks were disrupting pilgrimage routes through Asia to the sacred Christian sites. A series of crusades (military expeditions) set out from Europe over the next 200 years, capturing Jerusalem in 1099 and ruling the Holy Land until the crusaders were driven out in 1291.

The Black Death

In the 1330s the bubonic plague broke out in eastern Asia, spreading to the Black Sea in 1346. Rats on ships, infested with parasitic fleas, carried the plague to European ports in 1347, and it soon spread across the continent. By the time the plague died out in 1351, around 24 million people—one third of Europe's population—had died, causing many social and economic problems. Towns and farms lost their workers, prices fell, and wages rose as labor became scarce.

Scottish independence
Robert the Bruce's victory against the English at Bannockburn, in 1314, led to Scottish independence by 1328.

Bannockburn

SCOTLAND

North Sea

IRELAND

Tower of London
After his victory at Hastings, William built a royal home and fort beside the Thames river

WALES

Concentric castle on the Welsh border

ENGLAND

LONDON

Hastings

Battle of Hastings
In 1066 the Normans invaded England and defeated Harold II.

Agincourt

Normandy

English longbowman

Paris

Champagne

Poitiers

FRANCE

The feudal system
Across Europe serfs (peasants), dependent on their lords, worked the land in return for shelter and protection.

Vineyard in Gascony

Clermont

Santiago de Compostela

León

LEÓN

Spanish windmill

CASTILE

PORTUGAL

Pilgrimage
Christian pilgrims walked hundreds of miles to pray at holy places such as Rome, Jerusalem, and Santiago de Compostela.

Avignon

ARAGON

Lisbon

Muslim rule
The Muslim Moors controlled a small region in Granada, southern Spain.

Spain

Crusaders setting out for the Holy Land in the Near East

GRANADA

Granada

International trade
Venice and Genoa dominated trade in the Mediterranean, importing goods from as far away as central Asia and China.

0 ——— 500km
0 ——— 250 miles

SWEDEN

Neva

Sturdy Hanseatic cog (ship) used to transport goods

Fir trees

Novgorod •

The Hanseatic League
Thirty-seven northern German and Baltic towns formed a league that dominated trade in northern Europe.

Trade settlements
Hanseatic traders set up *kontors* (foreign depots) where their merchants could live and trade securely.

Salted fish from the Baltic

Hamburg •
• Lubeck

HOLY ROMAN EMPIRE

Germany

The Hapsburgs
The Hapsburg family conquered Austria in 1282. They dominated the Holy Roman Empire from 1274 until its end in 1806.

European assault
In 1241 the Mongols wiped out vast European armies in Poland and Hungary. They withdrew when their leader Ogedai died, saving Europe from conquest.

LITHUANIA

Kiev •

POLAND

Orthodox Christianity
The peoples of the Balkans and Russia were Orthodox Christians.

Banking
In the 1400s the Fugger family of Augsburg and the Medicis of Florence ran banks that lent money to local rulers and merchants.

Augsburg •

Wooden house in Kiev

Austria

Carpathians

Alps

HUNGARY

The Ottomans
The Ottomans from central Turkey defeated the Serbs at the Battle of Kosovo in 1389. They went on to conquer the rest of the Balkans.

Universities
The first university in Europe was set up in Bologna, Italy, in 1088.

Venice •

Balkans

enoa

Bologna •
Florence •

Kosovo

Black Sea

Orthodox monastery
Mount Athos in Greece was the most important Orthodox Christian monastery.

Rome •

The papacy
The Pope was the head of the Catholic Church. He was also an important political figure and owned a lot of land in Italy and France.

NAPLES

Constantinople •

Gallipoli •

Mount Athos •

BYZANTINE EMPIRE

SICILY

Mediterranean Sea

A.D. 1050
1054 Final split between Roman Catholic and Orthodox churches
1066 Duke William of Normandy invades England and seizes throne
1073 Pope Gregory VII increases authority of the papacy over secular kings
1095 Pope Urban II calls for First Crusade against Muslim rule in the Holy Land

A.D. 1100

1128 Portugal gains its independence from Spanish kingdom of León

A.D. 1150
1154 Henry II of England rules huge Angevin Empire, which stretches from Scotland down to Spanish kingdoms

1171 English begin to rule Ireland

A.D. 1200
1212 Christian troops win an important battle against Muslim Moors in Spain
1230 Kingdoms of Castile and León unite in Spain
1230 Towns of Lubeck and Hamburg form Hanseatic League
1241 Mongol invasion of Europe called off after Mongol leader dies

A.D. 1250

1274 Rudolph I becomes first Hapsburg ruler of Holy Roman Empire

1282 Hapsburgs rule Austria
1284 English King Edward I ends Welsh independence

A.D. 1300
1309–1377 Papacy moves to Avignon in France; major split in Catholic Church
1314 English defeated by Scots at Bannockburn
1337–1453 Hundred Years' War between England and France—caused by English claims on the French throne
1347–1351 Black Death devastates Europe

A.D. 1350
1354 Ottomans seize Gallipoli, their first foothold in Europe

1368 Lithuanians become Christian
1378–1417 Election of rival popes leads to Great Schism (split) in Catholic Church
1380 Hans Fugger sets up bank in Augsburg

A.D. 1400
1414 Medicis of Florence, Italy, become papal bankers
1415 English archers win major battle against the French in Agincourt

1429 Joan of Arc drives English out of France

A.D. 1450

A.D. 1500

Medieval Europe:
Castles and villages

During the medieval period, most people in Europe lived in small villages that were owned by the lord of the manor. Often, they died in the same village that they were born in and rarely traveled much farther than the local market town. Most people were serfs, which means that they were landless peasants who worked on the lord of the manor's lands in return for shelter and protection. The great lords of the country—the dukes and earls—lived in huge stone castles, heavily fortified against attacks by rival lords or invading armies. The first castles were built in France during the 800s.

A medieval village
This photograph shows Riquewihr, in France. A medieval village such as this was ruled by the lord of the manor, a knight who had been given the manor (estate) and all of its houses and fields by his lord. The lord of the manor served as the judge at the local manorial court.

Knights in armor
A knight was a mounted warrior who had been granted a fief (estate) by a rich and powerful nobleman in return for loyalty and military service. Knights were trained to ride and fight from an early age, learning their skills in jousts and tournaments. They followed an elaborate code of chivalry, which dictated their behavior both on and off the battlefield.

Siege warfare

Siege warfare became increasingly important as castles became better fortified. A besieging army had two options. The first was to surround the enemy castle and starve the defenders until they gave in. The second option was to try to force a way in, digging under the walls or breaking them down with battering rams, catapults, and (from the 1300s) cannons, or climbing over the walls with ladders or movable drawbridges.

Steep river cliff location, above the Wye river, to aid defense

Great tower begun in 1067, one of the first stone castle buildings in Britain

Inner defensive wall

Chepstow castle

The castle in Chepstow in Wales, U.K., was started in the 1000s. Medieval castles served as a residence for the local nobleman, as well as a military headquarters for his knights and the center of power in the region. The first castles were built out of wood and stood on top of a raised earthwork surrounded by a ditch, but later castles were made of stone and specially designed to withstand a siege.

Fortified gatehouse

Defensive ditch surrounds outer walls to prevent enemy siege equipment from getting close

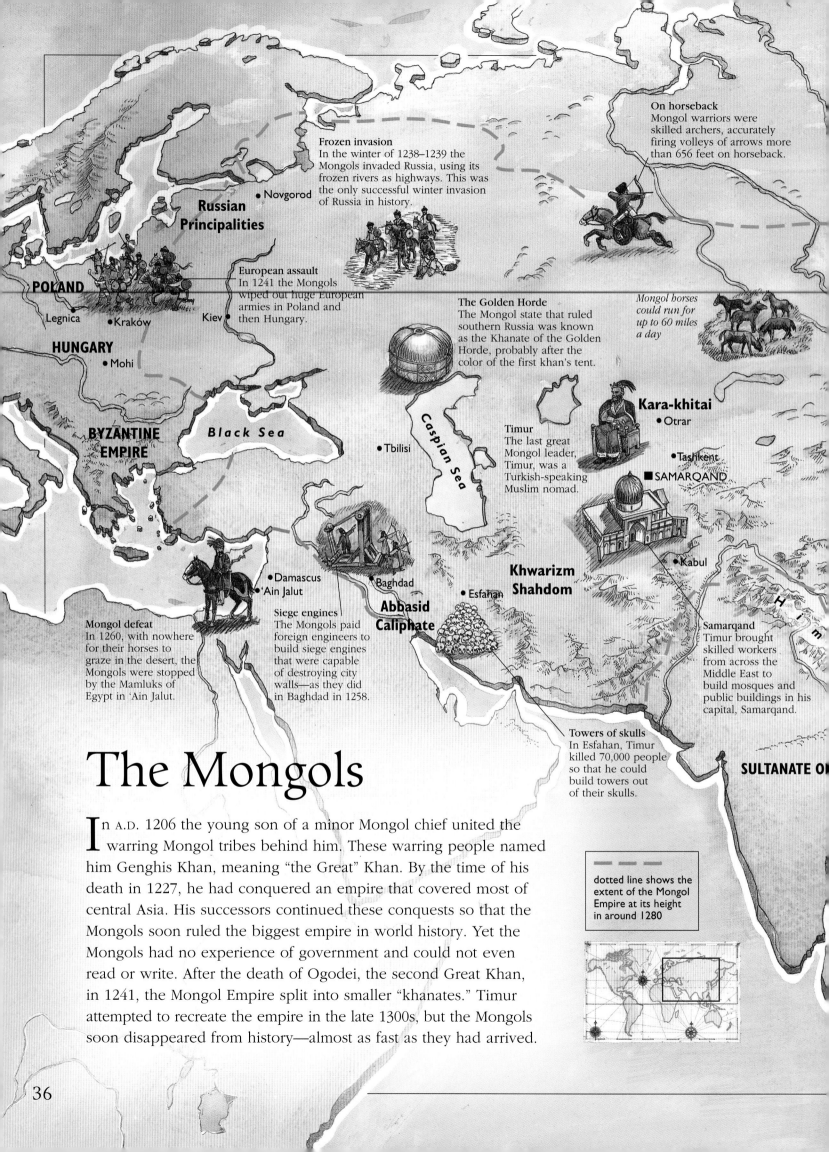

On horseback
Mongol warriors were skilled archers, accurately firing volleys of arrows more than 656 feet on horseback.

Frozen invasion
In the winter of 1238–1239 the Mongols invaded Russia, using its frozen rivers as highways. This was the only successful winter invasion of Russia in history.

• Novgorod

Russian Principalities

POLAND

Legnica •
• Kraków

• Kiev

European assault
In 1241 the Mongols wiped out huge European armies in Poland and then Hungary.

The Golden Horde
The Mongol state that ruled southern Russia was known as the Khanate of the Golden Horde, probably after the color of the first khan's tent.

Mongol horses could run for up to 60 miles a day

HUNGARY
• Mohi

BYZANTINE EMPIRE

Black Sea

Caspian Sea

• Tbilisi

Timur
The last great Mongol leader, Timur, was a Turkish-speaking Muslim nomad.

Kara-khitai
• Otrar

• Tashkent

■ SAMARQAND

• Kabul

Mongol defeat
In 1260, with nowhere for their horses to graze in the desert, the Mongols were stopped by the Mamluks of Egypt in 'Ain Jalut.

• Damascus
• 'Ain Jalut

• Baghdad

Siege engines
The Mongols paid foreign engineers to build siege engines that were capable of destroying city walls—as they did in Baghdad in 1258.

Abbasid Caliphate

• Esfahan

Khwarizm Shahdom

Samarqand
Timur brought skilled workers from across the Middle East to build mosques and public buildings in his capital, Samarqand.

Towers of skulls
In Esfahan, Timur killed 70,000 people so that he could build towers out of their skulls.

SULTANATE O

The Mongols

IN A.D. 1206 the young son of a minor Mongol chief united the warring Mongol tribes behind him. These warring people named him Genghis Khan, meaning "the Great" Khan. By the time of his death in 1227, he had conquered an empire that covered most of central Asia. His successors continued these conquests so that the Mongols soon ruled the biggest empire in world history. Yet the Mongols had no experience of government and could not even read or write. After the death of Ogodei, the second Great Khan, in 1241, the Mongol Empire split into smaller "khanates." Timur attempted to recreate the empire in the late 1300s, but the Mongols soon disappeared from history—almost as fast as they had arrived.

- - - -
dotted line shows the extent of the Mongol Empire at its height in around 1280

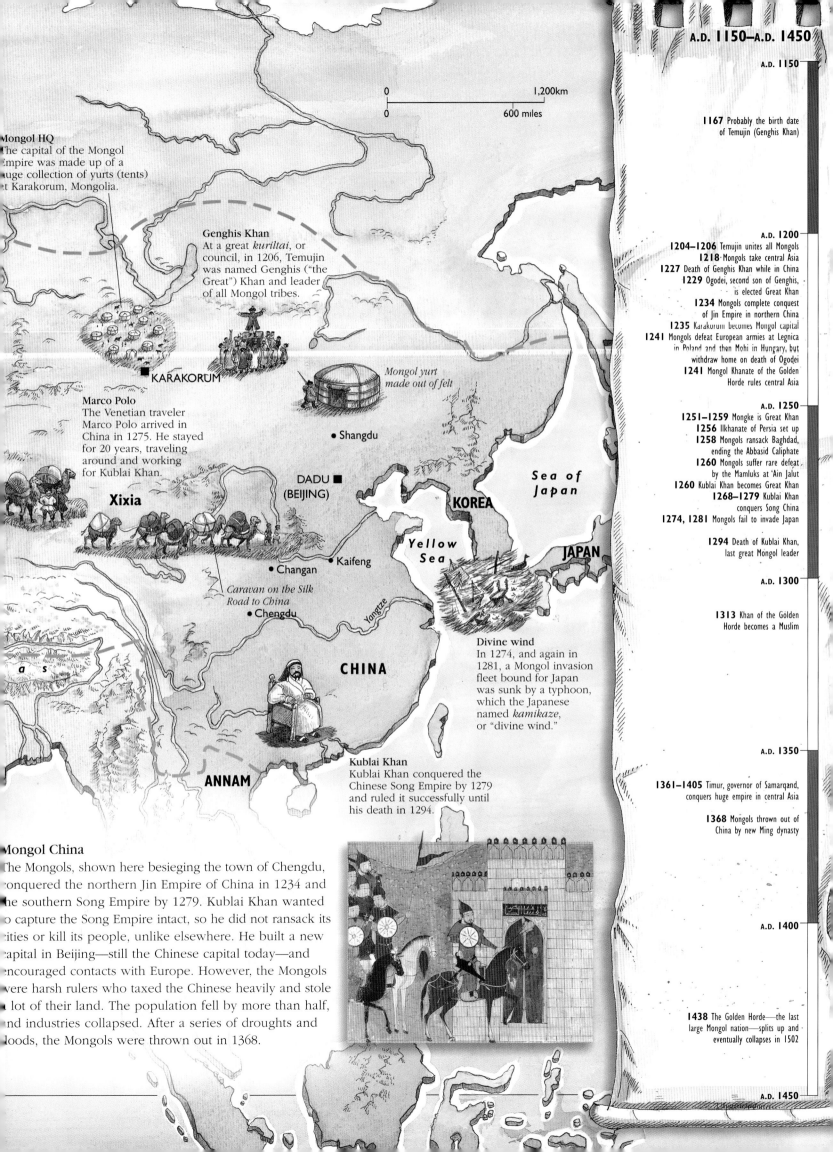

Mongol HQ
The capital of the Mongol Empire was made up of a huge collection of yurts (tents) at Karakorum, Mongolia.

Genghis Khan
At a great *kuriltai*, or council, in 1206, Temujin was named Genghis ("the Great") Khan and leader of all Mongol tribes.

KARAKORUM

Mongol yurt made out of felt

Marco Polo
The Venetian traveler Marco Polo arrived in China in 1275. He stayed for 20 years, traveling around and working for Kublai Khan.

• Shangdu

DADU (BEIJING)

Xixia

KOREA

Sea of Japan

• Kaifeng

Yellow Sea

JAPAN

• Changan

Caravan on the Silk Road to China

• Chengdu

Yangtze

CHINA

Divine wind
In 1274, and again in 1281, a Mongol invasion fleet bound for Japan was sunk by a typhoon, which the Japanese named *kamikaze*, or "divine wind."

a s

ANNAM

Kublai Khan
Kublai Khan conquered the Chinese Song Empire by 1279 and ruled it successfully until his death in 1294.

Mongol China
The Mongols, shown here besieging the town of Chengdu, conquered the northern Jin Empire of China in 1234 and the southern Song Empire by 1279. Kublai Khan wanted to capture the Song Empire intact, so he did not ransack its cities or kill its people, unlike elsewhere. He built a new capital in Beijing—still the Chinese capital today—and encouraged contacts with Europe. However, the Mongols were harsh rulers who taxed the Chinese heavily and stole a lot of their land. The population fell by more than half, and industries collapsed. After a series of droughts and floods, the Mongols were thrown out in 1368.

A.D. 1150

1167 Probably the birth date of Temujin (Genghis Khan)

A.D. 1200
1204–1206 Temujin unites all Mongols
1218 Mongols take central Asia
1227 Death of Genghis Khan while in China
1229 Ogodei, second son of Genghis, is elected Great Khan
1234 Mongols complete conquest of Jin Empire in northern China
1235 Karakorum becomes Mongol capital
1241 Mongols defeat European armies at Legnica in Poland and then Mohi in Hungary, but withdraw home on death of Ogodei
1241 Mongol Khanate of the Golden Horde rules central Asia

A.D. 1250
1251–1259 Mongke is Great Khan
1256 Ilkhanate of Persia set up
1258 Mongols ransack Baghdad, ending the Abbasid Caliphate
1260 Mongols suffer rare defeat by the Mamluks at 'Ain Jalut
1260 Kublai Khan becomes Great Khan
1268–1279 Kublai Khan conquers Song China
1274, 1281 Mongols fail to invade Japan

1294 Death of Kublai Khan, last great Mongol leader

A.D. 1300

1313 Khan of the Golden Horde becomes a Muslim

A.D. 1350

1361–1405 Timur, governor of Samarqand, conquers huge empire in central Asia

1368 Mongols thrown out of China by new Ming dynasty

A.D. 1400

1438 The Golden Horde—the last large Mongol nation—splits up and eventually collapses in 1502

A.D. 1450

African kingdoms

Trade in gold, ivory, salt, cattle—and also slaves—brought great wealth to the interior (noncoastal parts) of Africa. This led to the creation of several wealthy trading nations such as Ghana, Mali, and Great Zimbabwe. The West African states grew rich on trade across the Sahara with the Muslim world and Europe to their north. On the east coast, Muslim merchants set up independent trading cities that prospered by doing business across the Indian Ocean—with the Arabian peninsula, India, and China. Arab merchants introduced Islam to West Africa and coastal East Africa, while Christianity flourished in both Aksum and Ethiopia in the east of the continent.

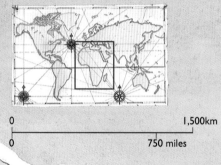

0   1,500km
0   750 miles

Portuguese exploration
After 1432, Portuguese navigators began to explore the west coast of Africa—in search of trade and wealth.

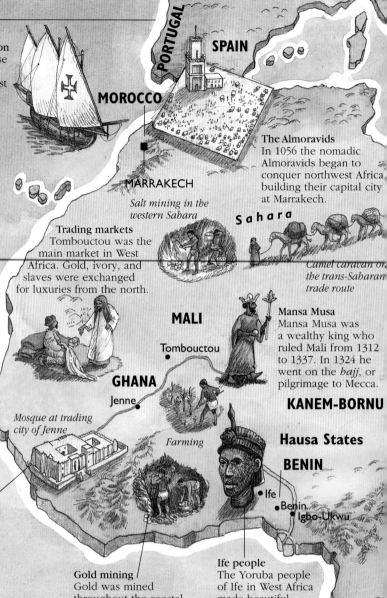

The Almoravids
In 1056 the nomadic Almoravids began to conquer northwest Africa, building their capital city at Marrakech.

Salt mining in the western Sahara

Trading markets
Tombouctou was the main market in West Africa. Gold, ivory, and slaves were exchanged for luxuries from the north.

Camel caravan on the trans-Saharan trade route

Mansa Musa
Mansa Musa was a wealthy king who ruled Mali from 1312 to 1337. In 1324 he went on the *hajj*, or pilgrimage to Mecca.

Mosque at trading city of Jenne

Farming

Islam in West Africa
Arab merchants from the north brought Islam into West Africa after A.D. 750, making it the main religion in the area by 1000.

Gold mining
Gold was mined throughout the coastal forests of West Africa. It was made into royal jewelry or traded north in return for other precious goods.

Ife people
The Yoruba people of Ife in West Africa made beautiful terra-cotta sculptures of their rulers and other heroes.

Atlantic Ocean

PORTUGAL   SPAIN

MOROCCO

MARRAKECH

Sahara

MALI

Tombouctou

GHANA

Jenne

KANEM-BORNU

Hausa States

BENIN

Ife
Benin
Igbo-Ukwu

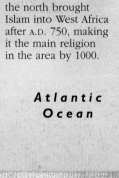

African trade

East African trade was dominated by a series of independent coastal cities, from Mogadishu in the north down to Sofala. These cities were mostly ruled by the Swahilis. The Swahilis were descendants of Arab, Omani, Yemeni, and Persian traders who had settled on the coast after 1000, bringing Islam with them. The rulers of these cities acted as middlemen between traders from the African interior and the Arab and Persian merchants who traded across the Indian Ocean. The vast range of these trading contacts can be seen by the presence of this giraffe in Beijing in 1414, a gift from the Swahili ruler of Malindi to the Ming emperor of China.

Cape of Good Hope

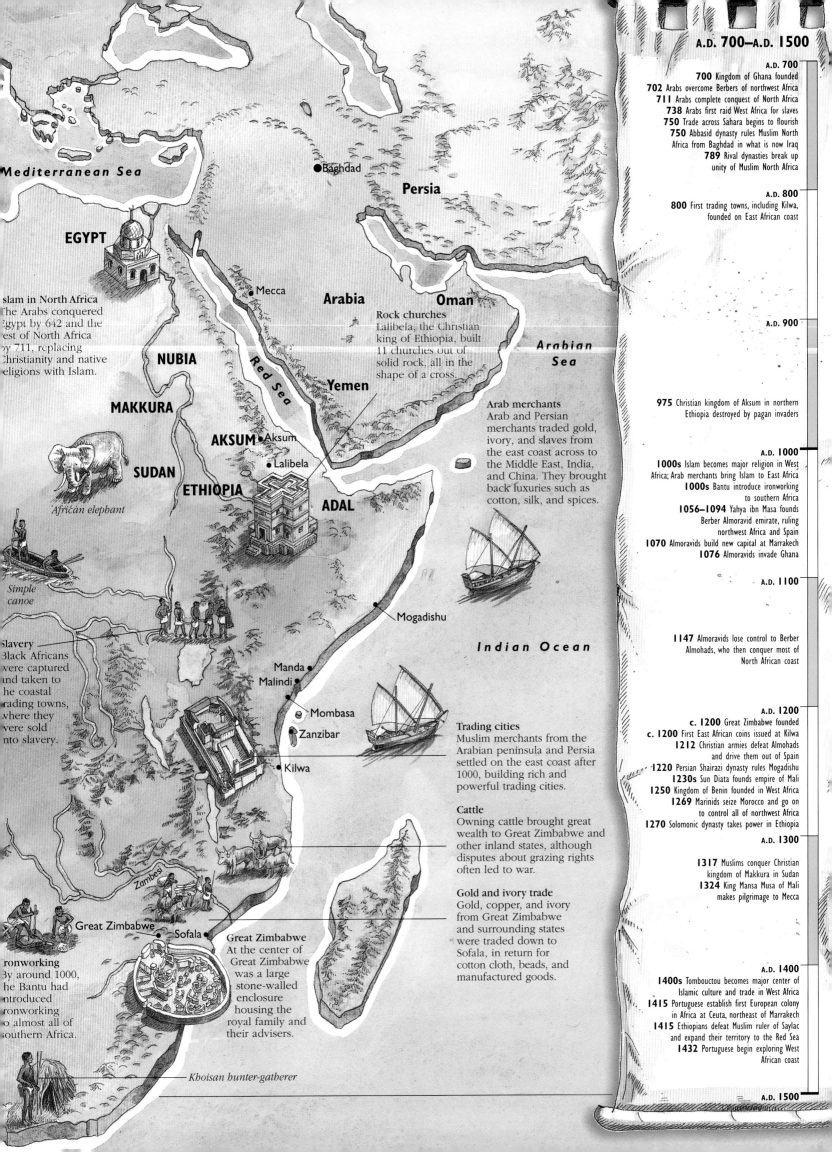

Mediterranean Sea

Persia

● Baghdad

EGYPT

Islam in North Africa
The Arabs conquered Egypt by 642 and the rest of North Africa by 711, replacing Christianity and native religions with Islam.

● Mecca

Arabia   **Oman**

Rock churches
Lalibela, the Christian king of Ethiopia, built 11 churches out of solid rock, all in the shape of a cross.

Arabian Sea

NUBIA

Red Sea

Yemen

MAKKURA

AKSUM ● Aksum

● Lalibela

SUDAN

ETHIOPIA   **ADAL**

African elephant

Arab merchants
Arab and Persian merchants traded gold, ivory, and slaves from the east coast across to the Middle East, India, and China. They brought back luxuries such as cotton, silk, and spices.

Simple canoe

Slavery
Black Africans were captured and taken to the coastal trading towns, where they were sold into slavery.

● Mogadishu

Indian Ocean

Manda ●
Malindi ●

● Mombasa

● Zanzibar

● Kilwa

Trading cities
Muslim merchants from the Arabian peninsula and Persia settled on the east coast after 1000, building rich and powerful trading cities.

Cattle
Owning cattle brought great wealth to Great Zimbabwe and other inland states, although disputes about grazing rights often led to war.

Zambesi

Gold and ivory trade
Gold, copper, and ivory from Great Zimbabwe and surrounding states were traded down to Sofala, in return for cotton cloth, beads, and manufactured goods.

Great Zimbabwe ● Sofala ●

Great Zimbabwe
At the center of Great Zimbabwe was a large stone-walled enclosure housing the royal family and their advisers.

Ironworking
By around 1000, the Bantu had introduced ironworking to almost all of southern Africa.

Khoisan hunter-gatherer

A.D. 700
700 Kingdom of Ghana founded
702 Arabs overcome Berbers of northwest Africa
711 Arabs complete conquest of North Africa
738 Arabs first raid West Africa for slaves
750 Trade across Sahara begins to flourish
750 Abbasid dynasty rules Muslim North Africa from Baghdad in what is now Iraq
789 Rival dynasties break up unity of Muslim North Africa

A.D. 800
800 First trading towns, including Kilwa, founded on East African coast

A.D. 900

975 Christian kingdom of Aksum in northern Ethiopia destroyed by pagan invaders

A.D. 1000
1000s Islam becomes major religion in West Africa; Arab merchants bring Islam to East Africa
1000s Bantu introduce ironworking to southern Africa
1056–1094 Yahya ibn Masa founds Berber Almoravid emirate, ruling northwest Africa and Spain
1070 Almoravids build new capital at Marrakech
1076 Almoravids invade Ghana

A.D. 1100

1147 Almoravids lose control to Berber Almohads, who then conquer most of North African coast

A.D. 1200
c. 1200 Great Zimbabwe founded
c. 1200 First East African coins issued at Kilwa
1212 Christian armies defeat Almohads and drive them out of Spain
1220 Persian Shairazi dynasty rules Mogadishu
1230s Sun Diata founds empire of Mali
1250 Kingdom of Benin founded in West Africa
1269 Marinids seize Morocco and go on to control all of northwest Africa
1270 Solomonic dynasty takes power in Ethiopia

A.D. 1300

1317 Muslims conquer Christian kingdom of Makkura in Sudan
1324 King Mansa Musa of Mali makes pilgrimage to Mecca

A.D. 1400
1400s Tombouctou becomes major center of Islamic culture and trade in West Africa
1415 Portuguese establish first European colony in Africa at Ceuta, northeast of Marrakech
1415 Ethiopians defeat Muslim ruler of Saylac and expand their territory to the Red Sea
1432 Portuguese begin exploring West African coast

A.D. 1500

Polar traders
Inuits and Norsemen from
Greenland traded ivory, furs,
textiles, tools, food, and
other items as far north
as Ellesmere Island
in the Arctic Ocean.

Arctic Ocean

Trapping caribou
Native American hunters
set up their camps by river
crossings. As caribou crossed
the river, the hunters
trapped and killed them
for their fur, meat,
and antlers.

Buffalo traps
Plains Native
Americans killed
buffalo by driving
them over a cliff
edge—a practice
that lasted for more
than 7,000 years.

*Hunting whales off
the Pacific coast*

Mississippi

Great Plains

**Medicine
Creek**

Cahokia

*Pacific
Ocean*

Chaco Canyon
This D-shaped,
four-story apartment
building in Pueblo
Bonito in the Chaco
Canyon housed up
to 1,200 people
in 800 rooms.

**Pueblo Bonito
Chaco Canyon**

Cahokia
Cahokia was founded in
around A.D. 600. A huge
dirt temple mound, used
for religious purposes,
dominated the city.

Shell carving
People in the southern
Mississippi river valley
carved shells with
religious symbols to be
used in ceremonies at
temple mounds.

Farming the plains
Small farming villages
on the Great Plains
grew maize, squash,
and other products for
food or to trade with
nomadic hunters.

*Native
farmer
in Mexico*

*Searching for
seashells*

*Gulf of
Mexico*

Chichén Itzá
Chichén Itzá, founded
in 850, survived as the
Toltec capital of the
Yucatán Peninsula until
it was attacked in 1221.

Tenochtitlán
The Aztec capital
city had a huge
temple complex
at its center.

Yucatán Peninsula

Toltec statues
The Toltecs lived in the Valley
of Mexico and their capital
city was at Tula. They erected
huge statues at the top of their
large pyramid temple in Tula.

■**Tula**

TENOCHTITLÁN

CHICHÉN ITZÁ■

*Mayan scribe writing
on folded bark*

Palenque
Tikal●

*Jaguar in the
Mayan jungle*

GREENLAND

Viking Greenland
Viking Norsemen set up colonies along the coast of Greenland, farming sheep and cattle. They also traded with the local Inuit people.

L'Anse aux Meadows
Norsemen from Greenland set up a small settlement on Newfoundland in around 1000, which survived for 20 years.

● L'Anse aux Meadows

```
0                1,000km
0          500 miles
```

Atlantic
Ocean

North and Central America

Across North and Central America, new and advanced civilizations emerged during this period. The Mississippi valley people built large towns and cities with enormous dirt temple mounds. Meanwhile, the people of the Chaco Canyon constructed huge apartment buildings, unmatched in size until larger ones were erected in New York City during the 1800s. Small farming villages sprang up in the eastern woodlands and on the Great Plains, while the people of the west coast lived settled lives fishing the abundant Pacific Ocean. To their south, the Maya and Toltec civilizations flourished in Central America until the Aztecs emerged to dominate the region during the 1400s.

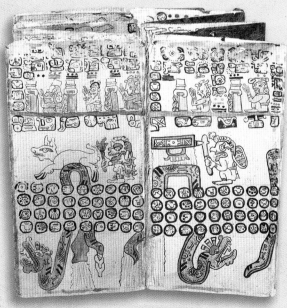

The Maya
The Maya were the only people in the Americas to devise a complete writing system. Their complex script was made up of glyphs (pictures), which represented both entire words and individual sounds. They used these glyphs to record the names and deeds of their families and kings on walls, pillars, and other stone monuments in their cities. They also made codices, which were books that were made out of bark paper coated with gesso (plaster and glue) and folded like an accordion. Only four of these books now survive, giving us a picture of what life was like in the Mayan civilization.

A.D. 600
600 Plains hunters now use bows and arrows to hunt wild game
c. 600 Cahokia founded in northern Mississippi valley

A.D. 700
700 Mississippi valley people begin building small towns with temple mounds
700 Farming villages flourish in the southwest regions of North America

A.D. 800
800 Hardier strains of maize and beans increase food production in Mississippi valley, allowing population to rise
050 Chichén Itzá, last Mayan state, is founded

A.D. 900
900 Toltecs found state with capital at Tula
900 Network of villages, linked by roads, begun at Chaco Canyon
900 Small farming villages spring up on the Great Plains
900 Hohokam farmers begin irrigating fields
986 Erik the Red founds Viking settlement in Greenland

A.D. 1000
1000 Permanent farming villages built throughout the eastern woodlands
1000 Viking settlement founded by Leif Erikson at L'Anse aux Meadows in Newfoundland
1000 Toltecs conquer Mayan states in Yucatán Peninsula
1000s Thule Inuits settle in Alaska and gradually move east, forcing out earlier Inuit inhabitants

A.D. 1100
1100 Towns with large ceremonial centers built in Mississippi region

1168 Tula is ransacked, and the Mexican Toltec state collapses

A.D. 1200
1200 Cahokia at height of its power, with more than 10,000 inhabitants
1200s Aztecs move into Valley of Mexico
1221 Chichén Itzá seized, ending Toltec rule in the Yucatán region

A.D. 1300
1300s Thule Inuits settle in Greenland
1300s Droughts cause decline of Chaco Canyon villages
1325 Aztecs found Tenochtitlán

A.D. 1400
1428–1440 Aztecs begin expanding empire under Itzcóatl
1450 Norse settlements in Greenland die out and are occupied by Thule Inuits

A.D. 1500

Central America:
The Aztecs

The Aztecs were the last and most powerful in a long line of peoples who lived in the fertile valley of Mexico in Central America. They were a warlike tribe who dominated the region after the 1200s, capturing enemy warriors in order to sacrifice them to their own sun god. The Aztecs were spectacular builders, creating huge cities and temple complexes. They kept elaborate records of their achievements painted on sheets of bark that were then folded into books.

The Aztec world
The Aztecs believed that the universe had been created and destroyed four times before the current "fifth creation" in which they lived. This huge stone, measuring 13 feet (4m) across, tells this story. The sun god is in the middle, with the four previous creations around him and then a band showing the 20 days of each Aztec calendar month.

Aztec religion
The main god of the Aztecs was Huitzilopochtli (above), the sun god and god of war. The Aztecs feared that one day the sun god would fail to rise into the sky and their world would come to an end. In order to keep the sun god alive, the Aztecs made human sacrifices to nourish the god with hearts and blood.

Daily life
Aztec houses were made out of adobe (mud brick) and often only had one single room. They were furnished with low tables and reed mats for beds. Aztec women cooked meals made out of maize tortillas wrapped around meat or vegetables such as beans, peppers, avocados, and tomatoes.

The Aztec capital: Tenochtitlán

The name Tenochtitlán means the "place of the high priest Tenoch." It was the capital of the Aztec Empire, and it was built on an island in the middle of a lake, connected to the shore by wide causeways. At the height of its power in the early 1500s, the city housed around 500,000 people and was much larger than most European cities of that time. Tenochtitlán is now buried beneath Mexico City.

Templo Mayor

In the center of Tenochtitlán was a walled precinct that was built for ceremonial and religious purposes. It was dominated by the Templo Mayor, a huge pyramid that stood 197 feet (60m) high. At the top were two shrines dedicated to Tlaloc, the god of rain, and Huitzilopochtli, the god of war. There priests made offerings and human sacrifices to the gods, placing the skulls of the victims on the walls of the two shrines. Each Aztec ruler expanded the Templo Mayor, building a bigger and more impressive temple around and on top of the previous one.

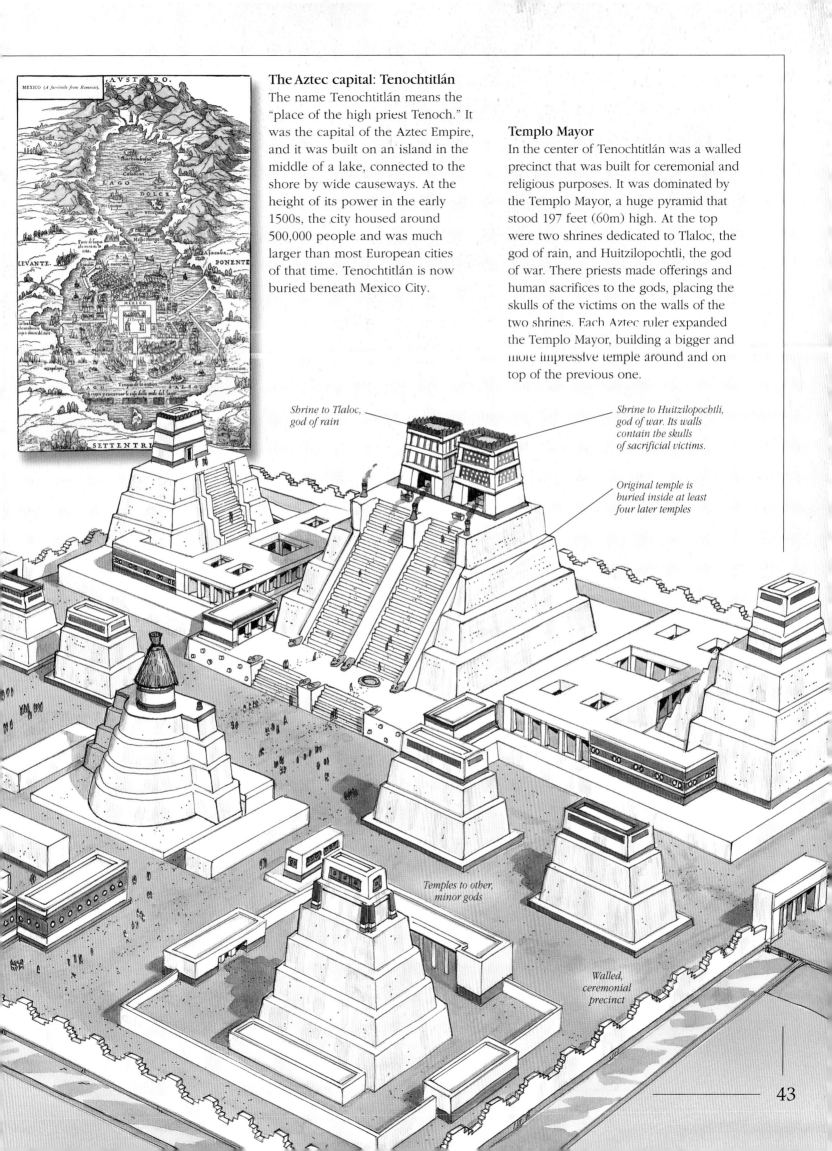

Shrine to Tlaloc, god of rain

Shrine to Huitzilopochtli, god of war. Its walls contain the skulls of sacrificial victims.

Original temple is buried inside at least four later temples

Temples to other, minor gods

Walled, ceremonial precinct

43

Chimús and Incas

Sometime around A.D. 1220, a semilegendary figure named Manco Capac founded the Incan state at Cuzco, high up in the Andes mountains, in what is now southern Peru. The new state was slow to expand, but in the mid-1400s it grew rapidly, conquering the neighboring Chimú Empire to its north and soon controlling 2,170 miles (3,500km) of Pacific coastline—from modern-day Ecuador in the north to central Chile in the south. The all-powerful Incan emperor governed more than 12 million people, keeping control through a powerful army and a network of fine roads along which troops could travel in an emergency. Efficient social services took care of the sick and needy, while everyone was expected to work hard to keep themselves busy and out of trouble at all times.

these lines show
the location of the
Incan roads

dotted line shows
the extent of the
Inca Empire in 1525

Incan scribes
The Incan scribes who
kept the quipus were
highly valued, as they
were the only people
who could "read" the
information that was
recorded in the
quipu strings.

Rope bridges
Rope suspension
bridges, made from
twisted vines and
wooden slats, were
hung across steep
ravines and wide
river valleys.

Terraced farming
Potatoes, beans, tomatoes,
squash, and other root
crops and vegetables were
grown on irrigated terraces
carved out of the steep
mountainside.

Alpacas
Alpacas were kept
for their fine wool,
which was made
into clothes, hats,
and rugs.

Textiles
All the South American
peoples were skilled
textile weavers using
alpaca and other wools
to weave clothes, rugs,
and wall hangings.

Chan Chan
Ten walled compounds
dominated the center of
Chan Chan, the Chimú
capital. Repeated
designs were carved
onto the walls.

Stone finishing
Incan stonemasons
finished off the
stone walls of
important buildings
by polishing them
with wet sand.

Sacsayhuaman
The huge stone fort
of Sacsayhuaman
protected the Incan
capital, Cuzco. It could
easily house all the
people of the city
during times of crisis.

Machu Picchu
The mountaintop city
of Machu Picchu was
a religious center and
frontier post. After
the fall of the Inca
Empire, it was not
discovered again
until 1911.

Oracle to the gods
With its temple and
oracle, Pachacamac was
one of the major religious
centers and pilgrimage
sites in the region.

*Harvesting a
potato crop*

*Sowing
maize seeds*

*Reed boat on
Lake Titicaca*

Quito

EMBAYEQUE
Valley

CHAN
CHAN

Moche
Valley

Andes

Pachacamac

Nazca

Machu
Picchu

Huá

CUZCO

Lake Titicaca

La Paz

Tiahuanaco

A n d e s

Roadside hostels
Rest houses called tambos, sited one day's journey apart, were built along the main roads to house messengers and weary travelers.

Food supplies
Food and clothes stored in the tambos were given out to the elderly, sick, and disabled during times of need.

Imperial messengers
Runners stationed at rest houses along the main roads carried messages to and from the emperor in Cuzco. A team of runners could cover 150 miles (240km) a day.

Pack animals
Llamas, the main pack animals of the Incas, were used to carry heavy loads at high altitudes.

The Incan emperor
The emperor was worshipped as the son of the sun—a living god. He was carried through his empire in style.

Fishing
Fresh fish that were caught offshore were carried by relays of runners to the emperor in Cuzco.

Incan walls
Stonemasons built walls using huge stones. The stones were so carefully shaped and fitted that a blade could not be placed between them.

Santiago

Pacific Ocean

1,000km
500 miles
0
0

Incan roads

The Incas were excellent builders, constructing a strategic network of roads that connected the farthest reaches of their massive empire to the imperial capital, Cuzco. The roads had rest houses called tambos, similar to the reconstruction shown here (left). The entire road system measured more than 12,400 miles (20,000km) long. These roads enabled the emperor to move his army quickly during times of trouble, as well as keep in touch with his regional governors through the imperial messenger system.

Strings of information

The Incas never developed a system of writing, but they figured out a way of recording facts and figures using a system of knotted string known as the quipu. Various colored ropes with single, double, or triple knots tied into them hung from a main rope. The color, position, and number of each hanging rope and knot recorded information such as the size of the food harvest, the amount of tax money that had been collected, and the size of the population. This was very useful during times of war or emergency.

A.D. 800

850 Chimú capital Chan Chan founded in the coastal Moche valley

A.D. 900

900 Sicán state founded in Lambayeque Valley in northern Peru

A.D. 1000

1000 The highland empires of Tiahuanaco and Huari collapse

A.D. 1100

A.D. 1200

1200 Chimú Empire begins expanding along the coast

c. 1220 Manco Capac founds Incan state at Cuzco in the Peruvian Andes

A.D. 1300

1370 Chimús conquer Sicán state

A.D. 1400

1400 Yahua Huyacac expands Inca Empire into neighboring Andes valleys
1438–1471 Emperor Pachacutec rapidly expands Inca Empire northwest to the Pacific coast
1470 Incas conquer Chimú Empire
1471–1493 Tupac Yupanqui, son of Pachacutec, expands Inca Empire south

1494–1525 Under Huayna Capac, Inca Empire reaches its greatest size

A.D. 1500

Index

This index lists the main peoples, places, and topics that you will find in the text in this book. It is not a full index of all the place names and physical features that are found on the maps.

Acknowledgments

The publisher would like to thank the following for permission to reproduce their material. Every care has been taken to trace copyright holders. However, if there have been unintentional omissions or failure to trace copyright holders, we apologize and will, if informed, endeavor to make corrections in any future edition.

Key: *b* = bottom, *c* = center, *l* = left, *r* = right, *t* = top

Pages 6*t* The Art Archive/Biblioteca Comunale Trento, Italy/Dagli Orti; 6*b* Corbis/Jonathan Blair; 7*tl* Alamy/Jeff Morgan; 7*tr* The Art Archive/British Museum, London, England/Eileen Tweedy; 7*c* The Art Archive/Viking Ship Museum, Oslo, Norway/Dagli Orti; 7*b* Corbis/Patrick Ward; 9*t* Corbis/Vanni Archive; 10*c* The Art Archive/Haghia Sophia, Istanbul, Turkey/Dagli Orti; 12*tl* Corbis/Archivo Iconografico, S.A.; 12*tr* Alamy/National Trust Picture Library/Oliver Benn; 12*br* The Art Archive/Bibliothèque Municipale, Dijon, France/Dagli Orti; 13*tr* Bridgeman Art Library, London, England; 14*cr* The Art Archive/Dagli Orti; 14*bl* The Art Archive/Bibliothèque Municipale, Castres, France/Dagli Orti; 17*bl* The Art Archive/Dagli Orti; 18*tr* Bridgeman Art Library, London, England/Louvre, Paris, France; 18*cl* The Art Archive/National Museum, Damascus, Syria/Dagli Orti; 18*br* Corbis/Archivo Iconografico, S.A.; 19*tl* Corbis/Patrick Ward; 20*bl* Alamy/Neil Grant; 22*cl* The Art Archive/British Library, London, England; 25*cl* Corbis; 27*t* Corbis/Christophe Loviny; 29*t* Photolibrary; 30*b* The Art Archive/Historiska Muséet, Stockholm, Sweden/Dagli Orti; 32*c* Bridgeman Art Library, London, England/Bibliothèque Nationale, Paris, France; 32*bl* The Art Archive/Museo del Prado, Madrid, Spain/Dagli Orti; 34*tr* Bridgeman Art Library, London, England/British Library, London, England; 34*bl* Corbis/Owen Franken; 35*tl* The Art Archive/British Library, London, England; 37*b* The Art Archive/Bibliothèque Nationale, Paris, France; 38 Los Angeles County Museum, California, U.S.; 41*bl* The Art Archive/Museo Nacional de Antropologia, Mexico City, Mexico/Dagli Orti; 42*tl* BAL/Museo Nacional de Antropologia, Mexico City, Mexico; 42*c* The Art Archive/Museo Nacional de Antropologia, Mexico City, Mexico/Dagli Orti; 42*bl* The Art Archive; 43*tl* Alamy/North Wind Picture Archives; 45*bl* The Art Archive; 45*c* The Art Archive/Archaeological Museum, Lima, Peru/Dagli Orti.

The publisher would like to thank the following illustrators: *Cover* and *page 1* Katherine Baxter; 19*b*, 35*b*, and 43*b* Mark Bergin; all other illustrations by Kevin Maddison.

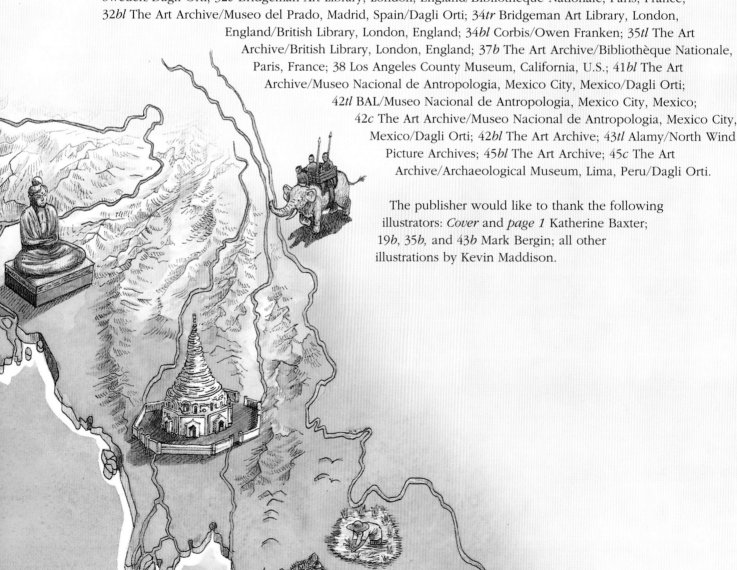